Should You Be a Teacher?

DANIEL DURKIN *and* AMY DURKIN

Should You Be a Teacher?

Daniel Durkin

ISBN (Print Edition): 979-8-35096-927-6

ISBN (eBook Edition): 979-8-35096-928-3

CONTENTS

PREFACE   1

CHAPTER 1: HOW'S YOUR TEMPERAMENT?   3

CHAPTER 2: REALISTIC EXPECTATIONS   21

CHAPTER 3: RHYTHM OF THE DAY   37

CHAPTER 4: THE STUDENTS   53

CHAPTER 5: THE PARENTS   69

CHAPTER 6: OTHER TEACHERS   85

CHAPTER 7: ADMINISTRATORS   103

CHAPTER 8: GOOD AND BAD ADMINISTRATORS   115

CHAPTER 9: HOW TEACHERS ARE EVALUATED   131

CHAPTER 10: "THE SYSTEM IS BROKEN!"   153

CHAPTER 11: CAN EDUCATION BE "FIXED?"   175

PREFACE

This book was written for anyone considering entering the ranks of teaching. Whether you are a high school student contemplating your next move in college, an Education major wondering what the next stage of your life will be, or someone thinking about making a career change, we hope our experiences in and out of the classroom will be of value to you. We make no claim to be educational gurus, research experts, or spokespeople for anyone other than ourselves, but are instead hoping to give two retired teachers' perspectives on what it is like being in the trenches of day-to-day teaching.

Although we make no claim to be experts in everything education, we do feel we are qualified to comment on the experiences of everyday teachers. Between the two of us, we have taught in an inner-city middle school, three inner-city high schools, and a suburban high school. We have taught all academic levels of classes, from mainstream classes to gifted classes. We have also taught a great variety of students, including students with learning disabilities, those with behavioral issues, those in need of specific emotional supports, those who struggled with reading or speaking the English language, and even those on parole. We have also written curriculum for five classes, including advanced placement classes. And finally, we also were involved in developing two online courses, including a "hybrid" course which combined both online assignments and classroom instruction. All told, we have a combined experience of over fifty years in the classroom. Despite our own experiences and what we've heard from other teachers in several different districts, we decided not to reference specific people, schools, districts, or even states because we do not want it to seem like we have an axe to grind and we want our views to be helpful to the largest number of people.

Our main goal is not to criticize the teaching profession and all that goes with it but to examine our experiences with a critical eye and not shy away from pointing out what we believe are both practical and systemic deficiencies in education. There are some serious problems with education, and you should be aware of what they are if you are to grapple with them successfully. Teaching can be an incredibly rewarding career, but you should go into it with as complete an understanding of the job as possible. We do not have any magical prescription for fixing all that's wrong with education, nor do we believe that such a prescription even exists, but it is important for prospective teachers to have a clear view of the challenges facing them.

Finally, if you do decide teaching is the job for you, we also hope you can use this book as a tool to shape specific practices in your classroom, without having to go through some of the trial-and-error we did. Beyond that, though, we also hope it will challenge you to think in greater depth about our educational system and your place in that system. We certainly do not have all the answers, but you should find that we raise some pretty important questions. And it is our assumption that questions are what keep any field alive and vibrant. We wish you the best in your teaching career and hope you will never be afraid to ask questions of your own!

Chapter 1

HOW'S YOUR TEMPERAMENT?

Introduction

For years, teaching has been a popular suggestion for students unsure about what to do after graduation, particularly for those students in the humanities. Whether you earned a degree in English, Political Science, or History, teaching seemed a good destination. Alternatively, experienced workers looking for a career change might consider teaching as a more worthwhile way to make a difference in the world than their current job. You might not have given much thought to the question of whether or not teaching is truly the right choice for you, but it's important that you do. You may have heard someone say, "If all else fails, I can always be a teacher," and maybe you've even said that yourself, but teaching is certainly not a job you should enter into lightly or because it seems like the least objectionable alternative open to you.

You might be thinking you have a good grasp of what teachers do based on the fact you were in school for all those years. If you are seriously considering going into teaching for the long haul, though, it's best to see the job in as high a resolution as possible, so it would be best not to overestimate your level of knowledge. It's one thing being in a classroom as a student, responsible only for yourself, and only making periodic eye contact with one person, the teacher. It's quite another thing to have responsibility for thirty-five students, each of whom has two eyes trained on *you*. If you're an older person considering a career in teaching, also realize the expectations for teachers are probably quite different than when you were in high school. Gone are the days when Coach So-and-So sat behind the desk reading a newspaper as you filled out worksheets. Today's teachers are expected to be far more active and engaged with their students.

Your perception of teaching might also have been influenced by how teachers are portrayed in entertainment media. These portrayals are too often inaccurate caricatures that follow a predictable script. Typically, teachers are shown as beginners assigned to the "bad kids." Despite not quite knowing what they're doing, these teachers somehow manage to overcome the students' initial rejection and quickly win them over. The teachers then buck the system in some way and deliver fantastic results. The message sent is that anyone who tries hard enough and cares enough can be a teacher. Although such stories typically carry a positive message, they gloss over the realities of teaching 150 or more students per day.

Even portrayals of teachers based on actual events often present an unrealistic view of teaching. A great example of this phenomenon is the movie *Stand and Deliver*, the dramatization of real-life teacher Jaime Escalante. In the movie, Escalante manages to get a class of low achieving students to pass the Advanced Placement Calculus exam. Throughout the movie, Escalante goes above and beyond reasonable expectations for a teacher, such as working well beyond his contracted hours, teaching on Saturdays, and even coming back early from a heart attack to teach. Although the movie takes certain liberties with actual events for the sake of drama, Escalante's real-life achievements were undoubtedly impressive and worthy of the recognition and praise he received. It must be remembered, though, his story is clearly the exception, not the rule. It simply isn't reasonable to expect all teachers to have the ability or the desire to sacrifice such a large portion of their lives for the sake of the job. It's been our experience that most teachers care deeply about their students and give everything they can. It's quite a lot to ask teachers to be some kind of superheroes, given the level of compensation and the lack of respect that goes along with the job. The lesson to take away here is that you shouldn't fall into the trap of letting preconceived notions get in the way of realistic expectations for your own teaching experience.

And finally, if after reading this book you decide teaching isn't for you, it's better to know that sooner rather than later. Even if you've invested four years earning a degree in Education or have spent a year and a half in night school getting a teaching certificate, don't feel obligated to get into teaching just because you've already invested that amount of time and money. In economics, there is something known as the sunken cost fallacy, which is simply the idea that it's difficult to abandon a course of action once you've invested heavily into it. Money and time you've spent getting that teaching certificate are gone forever, regardless of whether you move forward or not, so they shouldn't force you to take a job you know you'll be miserable in and will probably wind up leaving in a few years, anyway. As harsh as that sounds, it's best for your long-term happiness to be brutally honest with yourself.

What is temperament, and why is it helpful to know about yours?

Everyone is born with a personality temperament that affects how they interact with the world. Some people are just born wanting to be the life of the party, while other people would rather sit back and observe others. Some people are "worry warts," some are "social butterflies," some are "cold fish," some are "Debbie Downers," some are "sticks in the mud," and so on. All these labels refer to the person's temperament. At its most basic, temperament refers to how a person tends to respond and behave in given situations and around other people. As a teacher, you'll be dealing with thousands of people throughout your career in an ever-changing environment, so it's valuable to understand your natural propensity to react to those people and to that environment. Although not a fool-proof predictor of a person's behavior, the type of temperament they have will give insight into the kind of environments they tend to operate in best. Even if you decide teaching is not the job for you, it's worthwhile to have some understanding of your own temperament so you can pick the type of workplace in which you would be most able to thrive.

How can you find out about your temperament?

A helpful tool for gaining insight into your temperament is the "Big Five" personality model, which breaks personality down into five separate dimensions or traits. According to this model, personality can be categorized into openness, conscientiousness, extroversion, agreeableness, and neuroticism. In order to determine each dimension, people are asked how strongly they agree or disagree with a series of questions. An individual's responses to the questions are then compared to how others have answered the same questions. The person will then have a score based on how he or she compares to others. Since your score will be compared to others, it will fall along a spectrum, with most people scoring somewhere in the middle for each individual trait. The test isn't designed to delve into your very soul, but the traits of conscientiousness, extroversion, and neuroticism are germane to anyone considering a job in teaching, and we'd like to single them out for further discussion. There are a number of reasonably priced tests online that give a pretty accurate assessment of how your temperament compares to others, so you won't have to go to any great expense to gain some insight into yourself.

What the Big Five isn't

The Big Five model gives insight into your natural tendencies, but having natural tendencies doesn't mean you're a prisoner of factors beyond your control. Your thoughts, mood, and the situation you're in certainly all play a role in how you'll respond to other people and to your environment. Teachers come in all shapes, sizes, and temperaments, so you shouldn't be discouraged from being a teacher if your natural tendencies don't seem to line up with the vision you have of the perfect teacher. You can certainly compensate for your natural tendencies that don't mesh so well with being a teacher as long as you are aware of them and are willing to make certain adjustments to how you do things or how you view things. These traits also shouldn't be looked at as an all or nothing proposition. People are a combination of each trait interacting together, so you will never find a person completely lacking in any of the Big Five.

Finally, keep in mind that the Big Five personality model has nothing to do with judging you as a person. It isn't "better" to be high in conscientiousness versus low, or high in extroversion versus low, for example. There's a place for every temperament, depending on the situation. A lower score on any of the Big Five attributes is in no way demonstrating you aren't as good as others in some category or that you've somehow failed. For example, a Big Five personality assessment can identify those people who are more willing to take risks and those who are more risk aversive. It's not the case one is always bad and one is always good, since there are situations in life when taking a risk is the most appropriate thing to do. There are also times in life, of course, when being more cautious is the best thing to do. It's the situation that determines which approach is "best." There are times in education when you want to try some innovative approach to teaching even though it sounds like a risk. There are also times when you have to be careful to measure potential risks versus potential rewards. Students aren't Guinea pigs, after all.

What is conscientiousness, and how can you compensate if you're on either extreme?

The first of the Big Five personality we wanted to highlight is conscientiousness, which involves the degree to which you're organized, your general work ethic, and how diligently you perform your duties. Conscientiousness people will be present and on time for school, enforce school rules, keep proper records, submit paperwork on time, and strive to meet expectations. Every teacher is expected to plan instruction weeks and sometimes months ahead of time, sometimes for multiple classes, and usually have an endless stream of projects to grade, quizzes, and tests to give back, so some degree of conscientiousness is absolutely necessary. As a teacher, you have serious obligations to your students on a number of different levels, so your level of conscientiousness is certainly a trait you should consider.

Being on the higher end of conscientiousness certainly has clear advantages for a teacher. People high in conscientiousness are typically self-disciplined and don't need to have someone standing over them making sure they're completing tasks on time. You'll find once you've established yourself as a teacher, you will have a surprising amount of autonomy and may not see your direct supervisor for months at a time. Teachers high in conscientiousness also typically plan ahead, so students have a clear idea of what's going on from day to day. Having such clear expectations can certainly be helpful for all students, but it's particularly helpful to special education students, who seem to operate better in a more structured environment.

There are disadvantages to being a highly conscientious teacher, though. One disadvantage we've seen at various times is the danger of perfectionism. It's been said, "With a perfectionist, everything is garbage," and that saying certainly applies to some teachers. They are never completely satisfied with their lessons, their delivery, their assessments of student progress, or any number of things throughout their day. They also tend to be inflexible, which isn't a good quality to have in a job in which flexibility is required. Their work is normally of extremely high quality, but that quality comes with a price. Perfectionists put themselves under so much pressure to meet unrealistic expectations that they're more prone to burnout. We knew one teacher who spent hours working on individual lessons, hours on professional development, and hours on research. All of those things are quite admirable but can quickly leave you feeling overwhelmed. Overly conscientious teachers may allow teaching to consume their lives to the detriment of their own families and friends. It's impossible to know how many excellent teachers left teaching because of the undue pressure they put on themselves.

If you see the disadvantages of high conscientiousness in yourself, all is not lost. You just have to be aware when that trait is manifesting itself to your detriment and make some adjustments. One helpful strategy is to change your outlook and not to look too far ahead in your day, week, or month. Start by prioritizing the most important things you absolutely must accomplish for that day. If you don't prioritize tasks, then they all seem equally important, and not accomplishing any one of them will drive you crazy. It's perfectly fine to let some things wait until tomorrow, and you may even find what seemed like an emergency yesterday turned out to be not so important at all.

Another helpful adjustment is adding some flexibility to your thinking. Deviating from your planned lesson is perfectly fine if that's what's best for your students. For example, if students are truly struggling to understand a concept, there's nothing wrong with focusing on helping them understand it, even if it means you'll get a little bit behind in your unit. You'll also find it takes longer to teach some classes than others for a variety of reasons. You don't want one class getting a week ahead of another, but it's ok if one falls a day behind. The purpose is to teach the students you have in front of you, not to stick to some arbitrary timetable.

You may also find yourself on the other end of the conscientiousness spectrum, which also presents certain advantages and disadvantages. People lower in consciousness tend to be more flexible, for example, and can adapt more readily to unexpected changes in the daily schedule. Lessons will undoubted be disrupted during the course of the school year, so having the ability to roll with the punches and move on is a valuable trait. Also, since teachers lower in conscientiousness don't tend to hold themselves to impossibly high standards, there's less chance of burnout.

Part of the downside to being lower in conscientiousness, though, is that people with that natural trait are more likely to fly by the seat of their pants. They don't fall naturally into schedules and run the risk of being late to class, late for their duties, and maybe even late for meetings. Teachers lower in conscientiousness need to guard against procrastinating and be disciplined about setting realistic goals for themselves. That one class's worth of ungraded tests can quickly turn into a small mountain of "things to do" if a teacher isn't careful. It seems everyone has memories of that one teacher who took months to give corrected work back. With parental involvement seemingly higher today than it's been in the past for some parents, teachers with such a lackadaisical approach might very well find themselves having a very uncomfortable meeting in the principal's office. Advanced planning and organization don't come as naturally to people lower in conscientiousness as it does for others, but once again, it's not the end of the world.

You can certainly compensate for being disorganized with a little bit of forethought and planning. It would also be a good idea to set reminders for yourself in your phone so you don't miss important meetings or duties. Hopefully, you won't have to be reminded to go to your classes! Perhaps it would be helpful for you to have some kind of container where you could keep all the materials you need for class, particularly if you're moving from room to room. Several teachers we've known actually wheeled a cart from room to room and functioned quite well, despite being incredibly disorganized people. You would also do well to give a little more thought to where you put things. If you're sharing a room with one or two other teachers, they might quickly get annoyed if you constantly leave things strewn about the room or if you have to continually interrupt their class getting something you forgot. If this description applies to you, you'll have to make a conscious effort to get better organized.

It's also a good idea to set small, realistic goals for yourself if you're low on conscientiousness. For example, large, seemingly overwhelming tasks should be broken into smaller chunks as much as possible. Instead of trying to sit down and plan a twelve- to fifteen-lesson unit all at one sitting, break the task down into its constituent parts. Start with the final assessment, whether that's the students building a model, solving a series of equations, answering a series of multiple-choice questions, or whatever you think is appropriate to measure if they've retained the information. Once you understand where you're going to in the unit, break the unit into individual lessons, making sure each lesson takes the students one step closer toward the goal. Construct one lesson at a time, perhaps even setting a timer for fifteen minutes or however long you think you can do it and then simply stopping when time runs out. You might also give yourself a reward of some kind for each lesson you complete. It may seem easier planning a unit with the first lesson and then moving on, but in the end, there's a real risk of creating a unit that doesn't make logical sense and wanders toward some unclear destination. Students will quickly catch on to the fact your lessons are carelessly thrown together, and they will lose respect for you as a teacher. You owe it to the students to provide them with lessons that build on one another to a worthwhile goal, and you should certainly be able to justify why each lesson is in a unit to any parent or administrator who asks.

What is extroversion, and how can you compensate if you're on either extreme?

Another temperamental trait you should consider if you're thinking of teaching is your level of extroversion. Extroversion is a personality trait reflecting how you interact with people and the extent to which doing so energizes or exhausts you. People on the higher end of extroversion would dislike working in a cubicle all day by themselves, for example, while someone on the lower end of extroversion might function in such an environment quite well. It should be obvious a teacher is going to be surrounded by other people all the time and will be expected to talk to them and show some degree of interest in them, so if you are naturally shy or standoffish, it's important to give some thought on whether you'd be comfortable in the role of teacher. Remember, fundamentally, a teacher is a leader who must be comfortable interacting with, directing, and sometimes correcting, students. You can certainly learn to be more outgoing, but you also don't want to have to fight too hard against your nature.

One advantage of being high in extraversion is your natural tendency and ability to form relationships with a wide variety of people. If you're a teacher, it certainly helps to be a "people person," and interacting with students will be the highlight of your day. If you are a highly extroverted person, you'll also typically be more comfortable meeting new people than those lower in extroversion, so the first few days of a new school year or a new semester will be highly energizing and exciting for you. It's also interesting to note you may find your level of extroversion varies depending on whom you're dealing with at school. For example, you may feel perfectly comfortable in front of your classes but more reserved when talking with other teachers or administrators. All of that is perfectly normal. The Big Five temperamental qualities interact with and among each other all the time in ways that give you a unique personality.

Related to forming relationships with your students is your ability to create a cohesive and focused group environment in each class. Every class has its own "feel" that remains surprisingly constant throughout the year. You may have that sleepy first period class you have to prod to come to life every morning or that period right after lunch where students are bouncing off the walls with energy. Your comfort level with navigating the wide varieties of personalities and how they mesh together in an individual class will go a long way in determining whether teaching is a job you love or a job that gives you high blood pressure and ulcers. Highly extroverted people fall more naturally into the role of classroom leader who keeps the focus on the task at hand. They tend to thrive being at the center of attention and provide the enthusiasm necessary to be an effective teacher.

A potential pitfall for extremely extroverted people, though, is they may not make allowances for other personality types. If you see 150 or more students a day, it's guaranteed you'll have some students who are on the lower end of extroversion. You'll notice the extroverts in class will make themselves known rather quickly, but you're bound to have students who simply won't have the same need for social interaction as their extroverted peers. You must be careful not to fall into the trap of seeing the more introverted students as unfriendly or lacking interest in the class. It's only natural to feed off the energy of your more extroverted students, but it's also important not to play favorites or ignore the quieter students.

Another potential problem with being extremely extroverted is the danger of saying something without thinking about it first. Highly extroverted people typically like to talk a lot, and as a teacher, you certainly have to do quite a bit of talking during the day. It's important as an extrovert not to let your mouth get ahead of your brain. As noted, you'll have a wide variety of temperaments and personalities in your class, and there will definitely be students who dislike you intensely. Whether it's the way you look, the way you talk, or a dozen other reasons, some students will take an instant dislike to you from the first day. Such students may very well be listening for you to say something that "offends" them, and they'll set the bar pretty low. You can't be paranoid about every word that comes out of your mouth, but you might want to show more care than you're used to with your words.

It may seem being on the lower end of extroversion has no real benefits for someone who deals with people all day long, but that's not the case.

Introverts have their strong points, too, even when dealing with a wide variety of students. For one, introverts tend to be more thoughtful before they speak, so unlike extroverts, they tend not to say things that can be misinterpreted the wrong way. Introverts also tend to be good listeners and may very well thrive during one-on-one conversations. Students oftentimes just need a sympathetic ear, and a teacher more on the introverted side may be just what they need.

Despite such strengths, you may be concerned about whether you can actually get up in front of so many people every day and be the center of attention if you're more on the introverted side. If that describes you, you can compensate by considering the dynamic of being a teacher versus the dynamic of being a peer. It may help you to remember you're fulfilling a role of teacher. Students are not your peers, and you are in a very clearly defined, supervisory role over them. Your knees may very well knock together when addressing a room full of adults, but the situation is quite different when you're in front of students. You are the content expert, not your students, and the focus is on the material to be learned. If you know what you're teaching extremely well, and you certainly should, then you will have a greater sense of confidence. If you're still in doubt, it may also be helpful going over your lesson in front of an empty classroom while visualizing having it filled with students. That's a time-consuming process, but you'll find you'll always feel more comfortable going through a lesson the second time, so mitigating your anxiety will be worth the time commitment.

What is neuroticism, and how can you compensate if you're on the higher end of it?

The final trait we think is important for a would-be teacher to reflect on is neuroticism. Neuroticism is a person's tendency to respond to negative emotions, such as anxiety, depression, guilt, sadness, and self-doubt, and how a person responds to stress. Teaching is undoubtedly a high stress job, so you would do well to have an understanding of how you respond to stress and the negative emotions associated with it. Your level of neuroticism will also give insight into how emotionally stable you are, which is also a critical piece of self-awareness for a teacher. Although they probably will never articulate it, students have a strong expectation that their teacher is going to be the same person from day to day and not go through noticeable mood swings. That sort of expectation is completely unrealistic, of course, as everyone has trying days, but you should certainly give some thought to your emotional stability and make allowances for it, if necessary.

One actual advantage of being on the higher side of neuroticism is you may find yourself better able to empathize with your students. Teenagers are notoriously unstable in their moods and can certainly be prone to turning problems common to people their age into personal catastrophes. Whether it's them thinking they have no friends, they don't fit in, a certain teacher hates them, or their parents are monsters, you may very well find yourself better equipped to help such a student than someone who is lower in neuroticism. It might also be you've experienced similar thoughts, yourself, when you were their age and can be a valuable voice of encouragement to students who desperately need it. Oftentimes, you will find many students are in need of a good listener and someone who cares. You should be prepared to take on at least some of that responsibility as a classroom teacher.

Unfortunately, people high in neuroticism have a low stress tolerance, get upset or annoyed easier than someone low on neuroticism, and are more prone to self-criticism. High neuroticism, combined with high conscientiousness, can really make you overly harsh on yourself. You will definitely be your own harshest critic if you are high in both of those temperamental qualities. You might also be anxious about "doing something wrong," even if you can't identify a specific mistake. Extremely neurotic teachers run the risk of ruminating on those bad classes or negative interactions and reliving them over and over again, oftentimes even in their dreams. Even when not at school, their thoughts may continually go back to what happened during the day. One way to combat that sort of thinking is to remind yourself what happened is over, and no amount of worrying or reliving it can change it. Sadly, it's easy to focus on one negative thing that happened during the day while ignoring all the positive things that happened. One possible way of guarding against focusing too much on the negative is writing down all the positive things that happened during the day. As much as you can, put your focus on things that went well.

Another important thing to do is manage your stress levels as much as you can. Deep breathing is one way to help your body calm down. Whenever you get a chance, take a minute, concentrate on getting a few nice breaths, and remind yourself you're okay. It may sound banal, but you should also make sure you're getting proper sleep, your nutrition is good, and you're getting exercise. You should also be aware of taking care of your emotional health, as well. For example, if you're high in neuroticism, it may be quite beneficial seeing a therapist. A therapist will help you sort through your thought processes, be a sympathetic ear, and give you practical strategies for dealing with your stress. Although there's still some stigma attached to therapy, you should ignore it. There are no prizes for "toughing it out" or putting up with the most stress. It's also possible you may need some sort of antidepressant or antianxiety medication. We've known a number of teachers who were helped immensely by such medications, and you shouldn't look at it as any kind of moral failure or personal shortcoming. Don't tell yourself you can just slog through life, but get the help you need.

A final note about high neuroticism is you should change your perspective as much as you can and go easier on yourself. Realize there are unrealistic demands placed on you that no one could possibly meet on a day-to-day basis. It doesn't matter how stressed out you are about that test you didn't finish making or how angry you feel about that parent email you got this morning, when you're around kids, you're "on." They expect you to be enthusiastic and positive every day, so you have to be on guard for how you present yourself. Everybody has bad days, and you're sure to have your share of them, but try to focus on the fact you have a job to do. You have to a leader in your classroom, regardless of what's going on in your personal life. That being said, you also have to be gracious with yourself and forgive yourself when you fly off the handle at that class that can't seem to shut up for thirty seconds or that kid who, once again, refuses to stop bothering the person in front of him. Every teacher out there knows exactly what you're going through because they've been there themselves, so don't beat yourself up thinking you're a horrible person who made some kind of unforgivable mistake. Teachers are human, and every single one of them says or does something they regret later. Make amends as best you can for those kinds of mistakes, put them behind you, and try to do better tomorrow.

Concluding thoughts

Although the majority of people's temperaments would not preclude them from being a teacher, there are those cases when a severely mismatched temperament can be absolutely disastrous. An example of that involves a sad story about a student teacher. He explained he tried engineering but couldn't meet the demands, so since he "always liked history," he figured he "would just be a teacher." In order to put his situation in context, it's helpful to know the expectations for student teachers are pretty straightforward and follow a well-defined sequence. Student teachers come to you, their cooperating teacher, at the beginning of the year or the beginning of the semester and don't do much at first. It's a good idea to incorporate them as quickly as possible, though, even if it's something as simple as handing back papers so they can get to know the students' names. The ultimate goal is to have student teachers plan and execute a lesson of their own and, hopefully, take over full-time teaching duties for at least a couple of weeks. There's no timetable for this process, but most student teachers feel comfortable teaching at least part of a lesson within the first month. During the student teacher's stay, that person will also meet with a university or college supervisor who will examine lesson plans, sit in on some lessons, and give feedback on lesson preparation and presentation.

The student teacher in question, though, ran into serious difficulty almost immediately. He was extremely introverted and found himself unable to engage in any conversations with students. As a starting exercise, he was directed to simply stand at the classroom door as students came in and literally say the word "hi." He couldn't greet the students at all, despite being encouraged to do so multiple times with his cooperating teacher standing right next to him the entire time. He had no explanation for his lack of communication ability despite numerous conferences on it. Eventually, he had to be given a chance to at least begin a class, despite serious misgivings about his ability to do so.

As feared, his first attempt at starting class didn't go well at all. He stood at the front of the room for about ten seconds while the students were talking and then said, "Hey." The students continued talking, not noticing him, and after another twenty seconds or so, he said "hey" again. One of the students heard him the second time and asked, "Hey, what?" The student teacher responded with, "Listen to what I have to say." He had to say "hey" a few more times before students finally understood he wanted to begin the lesson, and then they quieted down. By this point in his tenure, he had seen his cooperating teacher begin five classes a day for several weeks, so there was really no excuse for his lack of verbal skills. Until he left at the end of the semester, he continued to simply say "hey" to start a class, despite being given several specific alternative ways to get the student's' attention.

He was finally given a chance to plan and teach his own lesson almost two full months into his student teaching experience, which is an unusually long time to wait. His lesson began in his usual mechanical fashion, but halfway through something extraordinary happened. It was clear by the midway point of the class he had run out of things to teach, and after several seconds of a panicked look, he began teaching his lesson over again, literally word for word. It was painfully clear to the students he had memorized a script. Students, bewildered, began looking at the cooperating teacher in the back of the room for some explanation. Being merely an observer during that class, the cooperating teacher avoided eye contact and let the student teacher continue. It didn't take long before students were snickering and talking to each other. The cooperating teacher wanted to intervene in the situation, but student teachers must be given the opportunity to deal with difficulties on their own. This student teacher simply ran through his script until the bell rang as the kids weren't paying attention.

Despite daily observations and coaching by his cooperating teacher, observations by his university professor, and both observations and counseling by the head of his department, the student teacher was never able to effectively communicate with students or soften his wooden demeanor. It was clear by the end of his teaching experience teaching was not the job for him. Thankfully, he decided on his own on his last day he was going back to school to give engineering another go.

His is an incredibly sad story on various levels. On a personal level, he had already committed four years of his life and four years of student loans in order to get a degree in education, a degree he would never use. It was also sad that he was completely out of his element. Despite his best effort, he was clearly more interested in things than he was in people, so teaching simply wasn't the job for him. What's shocking is how he managed to get through three full years of an education program without any of his professors recognizing just how grievously mismatched he was with teaching. We can't help but see that as a failure of his college program. It certainly is a cautionary tale to consider for anyone on either extreme of a temperamental trait; in this case, extreme introversion.

Chapter 2

REALISTIC EXPECTATIONS

Introduction

Just as having a realistic view of your own temperament is valuable before entering teaching, it's also worthwhile to give some thought to your expectations about teaching. A phrase to keep in mind is "expectation leads to frustration," meaning that the higher your expectations are of something, the easier it is to be disappointed. You should certainly be excited and enthusiastic about becoming a teacher. Teaching is a great job, so in order for you to go into it with as clear a view as possible, think about what you expect to like about teaching, the type of work environment you're expecting, your sense of the demands that will be placed on you, and how confident you feel your education classes prepared you to meet the challenges you'll face in the classroom. You'll never truly know how well your expectations match up with the reality of your first teaching job, but it will certainly make things easier for you if you at least give it some thought.

Realize the positive aspects of teaching

One of our assumptions is that since you want to be a teacher, you enjoyed school and did well in the subject you plan on teaching. It follows, then, that one of the perks of teaching is you'll not only have the opportunity to talk about one of your main areas of interests every day but also learn that subject in greater breadth and depth. Every year you teach, you should know a little bit more about the complexities of your subject and why it's of value to study. You plan on devoting a large part of your adult life to teaching a particular subject, so you must believe it's worth the time and effort to delve more deeply into it. Increasing your knowledge is also necessary because in order to teach a subject you really have to know it forwards, backwards, and sideways, if for no other reason than students will have questions. There will always be things you don't know, of course, and there's no shame in admitting you don't know something, but students will quickly lose faith in you if you're consistently unable to answer their questions.

Another assumption we make is that since your job involves learning, you value knowing more about a variety of topics and may even need a high degree of mental stimulation. Part of the enjoyment of teaching is having those familiar classes to teach but also having new challenges every now and again. You might be a Biology teacher assigned a class of Environmental Science or you may be a U.S. History teacher assigned to teach Economics or Psychology and find that it opens up an entirely new area of interest for you. Teaching those new classes will also keep your brain fresh and active and make your day and year more interesting. Students will definitely pick up on your excitement about teaching something new and hopefully feed off that energy. You'll also be modeling the concept of being a "lifelong learner," which is unquestionably one of the goals of education.

Besides the mental workout you get from teaching, another positive aspect of the job is you will never be bored. We've both been in jobs where we were sitting at our desk an hour after lunch, wondering how we were going to stay awake for the rest of the afternoon. You will never have those days in teaching because you will never have the same day or same year twice. Even though you'll be teaching the same students every day, young people's moods can change dramatically during the course of the day or week, so they always present you with something new. You may also consider coaching or sponsoring an activity or club, which gives you exciting opportunities to see students in a whole new light and interact with them in a different dynamic. It may be difficult to coach a sports team or something well-established, such as the fall play or spring musical, but schools normally have ways for you to get involved in an activity. If all else fails, you can start your own club or activity.

Students will also keep you young at heart with their unique culture and, at times, quirky interests. Even if you don't mean to, you'll find yourself well-versed in the latest slang, music, and culture. You might also find yourself, intentionally or not, using a little current slang in class, much to the delight of your students. It seems very few things are as funny as an "old" person using young people's slang, so have fun with it every once in a while. You may also find you become something of a folk hero by singlehandedly bringing back old slang. One year, for example, students had never heard the expression "old as dirt" and thought it was hilarious. If nothing else, you may find the exchange of different cultures invigorating and even entertaining. It's also the case that their enthusiasm can be infectious and lead you in a completely unexpected direction.

One such case of the unexpected involved a student who'd spent the summer working at the home of Henry Clay, an important American statesman during the Antebellum period. For some unknown reason, the class was surprisingly interested in her stories about the details of his life and his significance to U.S. History. Since it was an Advanced Placement U.S. History class, it was quite appropriate to spend some time on him. Henry Clay quickly became a sort of class mascot, with students bringing in a poster they made of him and hanging it on the wall. Since his birthday was right at the time we finished new material and were about to begin reviewing for the AP test, I decided to designate it "Henry Clay Day" and have the students plan a party in his honor. When the day arrived, I was shocked at what an extravaganza they put on. Besides lovely decorations, they brought in a variety of food, held a Henry Clay trivia contest that actually was an excellent review of important material on the AP test, and generally had a blast. Henry Clay Day became an annual celebration from that point on and expanded to include honored guests, such as the principal, other teachers, and even students who'd graduated who wanted to come back. It was a wonderful way to build a positive and cohesive class atmosphere every year, and it was all because one student had the enthusiasm to share one of her interests.

Kids will also make you laugh. You're going to meet a wide variety of interesting people during your career, and you'll swear that some of them are destined to be standup comedians. One student, in particular, comes to mind. He was a senior who liked to dress in leather jackets and big, heavy boots. He was pretty scary looking, and a couple of the administrators gave him a hard time about how his heavy boots might be used as weapons if he was ever in a fight. He quickly earned the nickname of "The Kicker," even though he was one of the nicest students in the building. Toward the end of his senior year, the principal walked by our room with a couple of very official looking visitors and stopped right outside the doorway. The Kicker asked if he could use the restroom, which didn't seem like anything out of the ordinary. As he walked by the principal, The Kicker said loudly, "I love you, man!" gave the principal a huge hug, and then walked away toward the restroom. Needless to say, the entire class was laughing and the principal looked thoroughly aghast. It's hard to say why students do some of the things they do, but little incidents like that can certainly make your day and might actually stay with you years after the fact.

Another positive aspect of teaching is that you will most likely have a family-friendly schedule and at times may even be on the same schedule as your own children. You'll definitely have part of June, all of July, and part of August to enjoy with your family and won't have to think about daycare during the summer months. One issue you may run into, though, is how early you start, particularly if you teach high school. It might be necessary to drop your own kids off at daycare before 6:30 a.m., which can certainly present a problem. If you're lucky enough to have a family member who can drop your kids off, then that's a real plus, but if you don't you should really give a serious thought on the logistics of getting your kids to daycare. The good news is that if you do have to be at work by 7 a.m. or so, you'll be able to pick your kids up before rush hour most days and not have to fight as much traffic getting home. Also, since you're home relatively early, you can help your kids with their homework before you're completely exhausted.

A final selling point of teaching, and perhaps the most important, is you will never have to wonder if you made a difference. Think about it. You may be teaching a future president of the United States, a future doctor who will develop a procedure that saves millions of lives, or any other of a variety of people who'll impact others in a significant way. Even though the vast majority of students you teach will never reach the pinnacle of fame or achievement in their lives, you can be assured what you do matters in ways you will rarely know. You might be one of the few stable adults in a student's life, and that word of encouragement you quickly forgot about might just help carry that student through the day. You might also find the student who gives you a hard time every single day might be the one most upset if you're out sick. There will always be those students who never tell you how much you mean to them.

It's also the case some students who really need you will never say a word about what's going on in their lives. One of those quiet students is illustrative of what such a situation might look like. He was one of those "average" students who're so easy to overlook, but it was clear he was despondent at the end his ninth-grade year. He seemed even worse at the beginning of the next year. After talking to the student over the course of three months, he finally confided that his mother had been progressively sick during his ninth grade year and had died over the summer. He was also upset because he feared he'd have to move and switch schools, which can be an incredibly hard adjustment for any child, much less a quiet one who struggles to make friends. This student was one of those kids who might have easily fallen through the cracks if one of us hadn't been paying attention. You have so many other students and responsibilities to worry about every day that it's easy to lose focus on any one individual child. Remember, though, for a quiet student you may be the one voice of comfort and sympathy so desperately needed. You matter.

Be realistic about the type of work environment you prefer

You may not have given it much thought, but it's also important to ask yourself some questions about the type of work environment you prefer. Teaching is a job where your life is ruled by bells, with a strict, predictable schedule, so if you're a person who enjoys setting your own hours, you'll have to make adjustments. Ready or not, when that bell rings students are coming into or leaving your classroom. You'll quickly get used to the rhythm and become an excellent judge of just how long each period is, but you should ask yourself ahead of time if you'd like such a structured day. You'll certainly have quite a bit of freedom as a teacher and have the benefit of doing a variety of interesting and challenging tasks, but your schedule is one thing over which you'll have no control.

You should also give some thought about the level of stimulation you prefer at work. Schools are not sedate places, so teaching is ideal for people who thrive in high-stress, high-activity situations. Remember, you'll have to enjoy this usually boisterous and ever-changing environment for the next thirty-five years or more, so it's worth your time considering what it's like. Don't be shocked if you have thirty students or more in every class, particularly in a high school. For years, research has shown smaller class sizes are beneficial for student learning, something any teacher could tell you, but schools have increasingly moved to larger class sizes in order to save money. We've both taught classes of thirty-six or more, and it only takes a couple of students to get an entire class rocking and rolling. You'll also run into plenty of excitement outside of your classroom. For example, one of us worked in an inner-city middle school, and during cafeteria duty, it was so deafening you literally had to shout in a person's ear to be heard. Believe it or not, we normally communicated through hand signals, facial expressions, and sometimes even written notes! As long as you're prepared to go into you job with the proper energy and enthusiasm, you'll find you might actually be energized by the exuberance of those young people.

On a related note, it's also important you like the age group you'll be teaching. Most of the people you'll be interacting with throughout the day will be your students, so be honest with yourself about whether or not you'd like to spend most of your day with that age group. One thing we noticed very quickly is there seems to be a great divide a between elementary school teachers and high school teachers. Elementary teachers always say, "I can't believe you can deal with kids that age. They look so grown up!" High school teachers typically say something like, "I can't believe you can deal with kids that young." Personally, we always imagined elementary school teachers being swamped with needy children with runny noses and no concept of personal space. There's a lot to be said for students who can use the restroom all by themselves. Realize, too, that if you're a secondary teacher, you might be teaching sixth graders or you might be teaching seniors in high school.

Finally, it's also important to keep in mind that you'll be working with or around other adults who are not teachers. Whether they're parent volunteers in the library, office secretaries, custodians, guidance counselors, security personnel, school psychologists, or parole officers, you should afford them the respect they deserve because the school wouldn't function as well (or at all) without them. Sadly, in some schools there's a real pecking order for the adults. For example, in some schools Advanced Placement teachers are on top, then Honors teachers, "regular" teachers, secretaries, security, and then custodians. In one school, a teacher caused an absolute scandal one year by having the temerity to eat lunch in the teachers' lounge with the secretaries. Apparently, the unwritten rule was that no teacher actually *ate* in the teachers' lounge but only in their department areas. It took weeks before the whispered criticism of several scandalized teachers came out, but apparently, it became known throughout most of the school. If you ever run into such a situation, you should avoid such childishness and appreciate that other adults in the building also have difficult jobs, too.

Understand the nature of the job, itself

One expectation you probably have, and a legitimate one, is how much money will you make as a teacher. You need to be completely honest with yourself about how much compensation is acceptable to you and to what extent you're motivated by money. You aren't going to get rich teaching, but chances are you'll be compensated fairly well, particularly if you were a History or English major with fewer higher-paying alternatives. Realize, too, you'll most likely go through a series of yearly salary raises before reaching maximum salary. How long it takes to get to the maximum salary varies according to district, but it's typically at least ten years. If you're expecting to make maximum teacher pay your first year, you're going to be sorely disappointed. Realize, too, that the maximum teacher salary for a district is most likely reserved for those teachers with a doctorate degree.

It's important not to focus simply on salary, though, because you'll be compensated in other important ways. For example, we both had outstanding health insurance coverage our entire careers. The premium will be deducted from your pay check, so it certainly isn't free, but your health insurance benefits may be substantial, particularly if you work in a larger district. You may even have vision and dental coverage, which adds even more to your compensation. Another major consideration besides salary is whether or not you get a pension. As with health insurance, your pension isn't a gift, but merely delayed compensation. You'll be paying into a pension fund your entire career and will reap excellent benefit from it. If you add in your health insurance coverage and pension, you may find teaching is well worth a lower take-home salary, so make sure you consider compensation in its entirety. You should also consider your temperament. If you're the kind of person who'd lie awake every night wondering if you could pay the mortgage if your income depended on a commission, you'd do well by having a more stable but lower income job like teaching.

Make no mistake, however, because you'll no doubt earn every cent of that compensation. For one thing, teaching is not a 9-to-5 job and certainly isn't the right fit for clock-watchers. If you're a first-year teacher, in particular, you're going to come in early, stay late, take things home with you at night, and work weekends. You should also keep in mind your workday starts early, very early if you're a high school teacher. And don't be deceived by how early you start, thinking you'll have those fifteen minutes to grab a cup of coffee and have a leisurely chat with your coworker about last night's game. You may well find yourself with ten emails, three voice messages requiring a quick response, or unexpected visitors when you're trying to get ready for the day, so plan accordingly. It's fairly common for a student to come in with a question, someone to ask you for a week's worth of work for a student who's in detention, or for some panicked person who forgot to give you that form you-have-to-fill-out-by-8am-today to cross your path, so arriving earlier than your official start time is usually a very good idea.

If there's anything you might have unrealistic expectations about, we hope it isn't the amount of encouragement you'll get. You need to be realistic about the job and understand that encouragement will be sparse. Every now and then you'll get the uplifting word or note, but the majority of what you'll get is criticism, whether if it's from students, administrators, or parents. Students typically complain about the lesson. Hearing "this isn't fun," "this is stupid," or "why do we have to do this?" begins to wear on you after about the nine hundredth time and adds to a negative tone for the class. It can be very difficult to do at times, but realize student complains are part of the job and shouldn't be taken personally. Parents will inevitably have their complaints, as well, typically about grades. Once again, take it as part of the job and not a personal statement on you, regardless of how personal and unfair the complaints sound. Some parents blame teachers for their child's lack of achievement, regardless of the circumstances, so be prepared for that and make sure your grading system is valid and fair. Administrators, too, can have their share of negative feedback. The way teachers are evaluated has changed (more on that later), but don't be shocked if you get no positive feedback after a formal class observation. Between the two of us, we can only remember one positive comment by an administrator in our final ten years of teaching. If being praised for a job well done is important to you, you must adjust your expectations if you're to make it until retirement.

Related to the general paucity of encouragement in teaching is the fact that you'll never truly see the fruits of your labor. There's definitely a sense of satisfaction when you can see the end product of all your efforts, whether it's that room you finally got painted, that lawn you just mowed, or any other number of tasks with a clear ending point. With teaching, there's a satisfaction (more of a relief!) when the year is finally over, but seeing your students walk out of the door wasn't the purpose of all your effort. You will rarely know what kind of impact you had on them, so you have to be okay with that reality. You can probably see it in your own experiences. How many times have you thought fondly about a teacher who made a difference in your life but never let that teacher know? Maybe it's because you worry too many years have gone by or you're afraid the teacher won't remember you, but who knows how many of your former students will think about you in the same way? We're assuming almost all people need to know they've served some sort of purpose in their working lives, so don't be shy about reminding yourself of the good you've done if you ever wonder if you're making a difference.

Another critical reality of teaching, and one you should expect and accept, is you have serious legal and moral obligations to your students. Your education program will most likely acquaint you with the concept of *in loco parentis*. *In loco parentis* is a Latin term meaning "in place of a parent" or "instead of a parent." You don't have all the same responsibilities of a parent, obviously, but you are, in effect, standing in the place of a student's parents while that student is in your school. Take this legal and moral responsibility seriously. Keep in mind you are also an official representative of your school district and its community members, so always look out for what's in the best interest of all children in your school. One obvious example of a legal and moral obligation involves suspected child abuse. You are legally obligated to report suspected child abuse to your school administration immediately. We would also highly recommend you report suspected child abuse directed to your state, even if that isn't a requirement. When it comes to the safety and health of your students, there's no such thing as being too cautious. Your responsibility to students doesn't end at your classroom door, either. The general safety of all students, anywhere in the building you encounter them, is clearly your shared responsibility with the other adults.

Lastly, and most significantly, teaching is by its very nature an extremely stressful job, particularly if you work in an inner-city school, so expect that. Teacher burnout is very real, and at least part of the stress is physical. Realize you'll probably be doing quite a bit of talking and quite a bit of standing, both during class and while on duty (e.g., cafeteria duty). You may also find yourself working in a building with no air conditioning. We've both been in rooms where the temperature registered 85° by 7:30 a.m. and both have known teachers who've collapsed from the heat. You may also develop high blood pressure and/or ulcers from the stress. We know one teacher whose blood pressure became so dangerously high she was taken to the hospital during school hours and afterwards had to have her blood pressure checked daily by the school nurse. Those physical demands, especially as you get older, really take a toll, so it's important you take care of yourself.

Far more than being physically taxing, you should also expect some teaching jobs to put you through the psychological wringer on a daily basis for various reasons. One reason why is there's a very real expectation you're going to be teaching at the top of your game every single day, regardless of whether you're sick, exhausted, or have absolute catastrophes going on in your personal life. You'll also be facing a constant series of deadlines that have to be met exactly on time and will be expected to keep an incredible amount of paperwork. You'll find quite a bit of your non-class time will be spent filling out various school and district forms that must be completed with 100 percent accuracy. For example, if one day you forget to submit a class's attendance or make any kind of error, you're bound to receive some kind of official-sounding warning. Besides pressing deadlines, though, are Individualized Education Programs (IEPs) for special education students. IEPs are binding legal documents that must be followed to the letter, and you may find yourself dealing with dozens of them every day, each with specialized demands. It's critical you be as faithful in fulfilling your duties as possible, but you should also realize that every mistake you make will most likely be highlighted, scrutinized, and documented.

Adding to your stress is the fact that your level of responsibility is wildly out of proportional to your level of control. You have no idea what types of students are going to walk through your door every year, but you're held responsible for how well they do on standardized tests. You may have a student who doesn't come to school until early October or only shows up in your class twice all year, but if that student doesn't perform proficiently on a test, you're the one who gets the blame. The same is true if you have eight or nine unruly students who make it nearly impossible for you to teach every day. You're also at the mercy of unexpected changes in the daily schedule and are simply expected to somehow "adjust." If the principal decides to have a last-minute pep rally during your Algebra test and then asks you why you're behind in teaching the curriculum, it can be an extremely frustrating experience. You might also have little to no control over your curriculum, either, and may even be required to teach a scripted curriculum. In such a curriculum, you are required to move through lessons at a defined pace, regardless of whether the students understand the concepts. If that curriculum proves unsuccessful, you will still be the one held responsible for its failure. There seems to be a popular notion that teachers simply teach whatever they want, but that clearly isn't the case.

Are bad teachers protected by tenure?

We have heard, and most likely you have, as well, some people say something akin to, "Teachers have tenure, so you can't get rid of the bad ones." That statement is inaccurate, so you do not have an ironclad job for life once you become a teacher. We think the confusion over the term "tenure" probably stems from the fact that the same term is used to describe both college professors and noncollege level teachers, even though the term means very different things. "Tenure," for our purposes, simply means the school district and the teachers' union have agreed there's a well-defined process when it comes to the evaluation, discipline, and termination of teachers who've worked for the district for a certain number of years. The purpose of tenure is to make sure teachers aren't simply dismissed for arbitrary reasons. It does *not* mean a teacher can't be fired. In our experience, if a teacher was not performing the job adequately, an administrator would sit down with the teacher, point out the deficiency in question, and work out a plan to correct that deficiency. If the teacher still didn't improve, there was another meeting to discuss why there was no improvement. After that, if the teacher still was unable to correct the identified problem, that teacher would receive an unsatisfactory rating for the semester. After receiving an unsatisfactory rating for two consecutive semesters, that teacher could then be terminated.

The idea of teacher tenure, if you think about it from a business perspective, benefits both the school district and the teacher. It's difficult and time-consuming to find and train skilled employees, especially if those employees have been with an organization for five years or more, so it's in a school district's best interest to improve their current employees rather than start from scratch and hope the new ones are better. Besides that, a school district doesn't want to develop the reputation of constantly going through employees. A high turnover rate is a definite red flag for potential applicants and may even be fatal for a district struggling to recruit and retain employees. It's also not in the best interest of students to have their teachers going through a revolving door. Unfortunately, both of us have encountered teachers who should've been relieved of their duties but have found administrators simply haven't gone through the process it takes to remove such teachers. The process is certainly there, though, but it only works when administrators take the time and effort to implement it.

Concluding thoughts

Given all the challenges of teaching, you may be asking yourself if your education program has truly prepared you for what's to come. It isn't possible for any education program to fully prepare you for your potential experiences in the classroom, so it's helpful not to have an exaggerated sense of how well you're prepared to step into that classroom. This is in no way a criticism of education programs, generally, but simply an acknowledgement of fact. Part of the limitations of teacher preparation is that every school presents a unique set of challenges, but it's also been our experience, both in our own graduate courses and through conversations with student observers, that some of the faculty of education programs simply lack the experience and expertise to train the next generation of teachers. It's also fair to wonder whether what is focused on in education programs has direct applicability to the type of classrooms their students will be entering.

While taking graduate courses, ourselves, we quickly picked up on the fact that the vast majority of people teaching those courses had little or no actual classroom experience below the college level. Out of all our combined graduate courses, in fact, only two of the instructors were currently teaching, both in high schools. The few others who'd spent time in a pre-college classroom hadn't been there in at least ten years. One instructor hadn't been in an actual classroom in thirty years. The most valuable courses, and those taught by actual teachers, focused on the practicalities of constructing unit plans, lesson plans, and the challenges of classroom management. Some of the other courses, though, were of no real value and often had good intentioned instructors who were clearly out of their depth. One such instructor, in particular, proved to be the worst teacher we ran across in our entire careers. Despite her staggering lack of knowledge and professionalism, this same person showed up later as an expert during an in-service day years after one of us had had the misfortune of taking her course!

Based on what we've heard from current Education students and other teachers, it doesn't seem like much has changed in terms of the quality of the faculty, but there does seem to have been a change of focus in the programs, themselves. For example, your teacher training most likely included old standby courses, such as child or adolescent psychology, the history of education, an overview of pedagogical approaches, educational research, and educational measurement and testing. Your program may also have very well emphasized referencing federal and state standards for education in your lesson plans. The student observers we talked to said their programs' first concern about any lesson plan was whether it met as many vaguely worded standards as possible. Based on these conversations, we wonder if the focus of lesson planning has shifted from choosing the most effective methods of reaching the learners to focusing on hitting just the right number of standards.

Another focus of current education programs is on "data-driven instruction." How that came to our attention with Education students was when one of them was observing a class. We noticed this student was trying desperately to type down every word we said, every gesture, how many times we walked to the right side of the classroom, and other miniscule details. The student later explained she was told to take such specific notes in order to collect "data." In all fairness, this focus is valid since administrators do the same thing when they conduct a formal observation, but we question the value of creating a verbatim transcription of a lesson. Is the purpose of an education student observing a veteran teacher to get a sense of the structure, rhythm, and practice of teaching, or is it to train them to be court stenographers? We presume this approach is used because administrators are desperate to quantify aspects of teaching, but teaching, by its very nature, doesn't lend itself to being broken down completely into measurable parts. A further irony is our experience has been many administrators are rather limited in their math skills and have only a rudimentary understanding of statistics and how they're used. Ultimately, you have to work within the system you're given, but if the approach of your education program has you asking questions about its effectiveness, that's not a bad thing at all. You don't want to feel completely unprepared, but a healthy skepticism of whether or not you're fully prepared to step into the job is perfectly appropriate.

Chapter 3
RHYTHM OF THE DAY

Introduction

Just as you should be realistic about the nature of the job and how well you're prepared for teaching, it's also important to have both some sense of the hiring process and the rhythm of your day once you begin as a teacher. Individual experiences vary greatly, of course, but there are certain commonalities when it comes to how the days move along, especially for teachers just starting out. Our hope in this chapter is to give you a look into those commonalities and the general pace of your day. We will also provide you with specific suggestions for structuring your individual days in order to help you acclimate to teaching. This chapter will also provide an overview of classroom management and what it means to be a "professional."

What happens before you're hired?

So, you've just earned your teaching certificate, have a good sense of your temperament and the type of work environment you want, and you're ready to dive into teaching. The first step is getting hired, of course, which begins with the important but rather mundane task of getting your credentials and recommendations online. There's no magical formula here; just make sure you follow proper conventions in writing and present yourself in the best possible light. You should also be prepared to answer standard interview questions, such as how you'll differentiate instruction for various abilities and interest levels of students. The only thing we'd advise you to do that you may not have thought of is research the district with whom you're interviewing. You should have questions demonstrating you're familiar with the district and the challenges facing it. Displaying knowledge of the district shows both your preparation and professionalism, so don't underestimate how important that might be in getting you hired.

Another step usually associated with getting hired as a permanent teacher is substitute teaching. You might be lucky enough to get hired on straight away, but you also might be hired on as a substitute teacher, either day-to-day or as a "permanent" or long-term substitute. Ideally, you'll get hired as a long-term substitute, meaning you'll have at least several weeks in the same classroom or may even find yourself there for a whole semester or an entire year. If you are hired as a long-term substitute, you should really treat it as one long job interview. Administrators will be keeping an eye on you and listening for comments or complaints from the students. If you do a good job as a long-term substitute, your chances of being hired on full-time are much greater. It's easier for administrators to hire someone known to them than take a chance on another job applicant who isn't. You should also be prepared for disappointment, though. We've noticed there's a perverse incentive in some districts to *not* hire really good substitute teachers since it's more difficult for them to find substitute teachers than it is to find permanent teachers. Being a substitute may indeed help you get hired, then, but there's certainly no guarantee of that. Districts obviously look at other things, such as what college you went to, what life experiences you bring to the table, and how well you interview, so don't give up hope if you're never hired on as a long-term sub.

If you do wind up substitute teaching on a day-to-day basis, be aware you'll run into some frustrating situations. You'll want to make a good impression as a substitute teacher, but you should temper your expectations about how much actual teaching you'll do. Some teachers won't leave lesson plans, while others will tell you to show a video that's no longer available online. Other teachers may leave you a full one-page, single-spaced note on what to do. That can be quite helpful, but if you're arriving at the same time as the students, you won't have time to read through such a long note while keeping any semblance of order in the classroom. All of these things and a dozen others can happen, so just prepare yourself for them, take a deep breath, and do your best. The students, themselves, will also likely pose a challenge. If you're lucky, the students will at least be cooperative even if they don't work as hard as they would for their regular teacher. You should be prepared, though, for anything.

One of us taught for several months as a substitute before getting hired and had an absolutely nightmarish first day at a middle school. One of the classes, in particular, was sheer chaos. Two students were trying to carry the teacher's desk out of the room, one student was crawling on the floor biting other students, another student was running around the room stabbing people with a long needle, and another student was in the back of the classroom selling drugs! When an administrator finally showed up fifteen minutes after the emergency button had been pushed, she simply talked to the two students in the hallway, had them bring the teacher's desk back into the room, and then walked away without ever coming into the classroom. Mercifully, the bell rang and the rest of the day wasn't quite as chaotic. Needless to say, that school was crossed off as a possibility for either another day as a substitute or as a permanent teacher. Some of you may doubt things were really *that* bad, but rest assured everything about that experience has been related exactly as it happened. The moral of the story is you have to decide for yourself whether the trials and tribulations of being a substitute are worth it to you.

What's it like when you first start as a teacher?

You've probably already figured it out, but keep in mind you're going to have to be patient when looking for a teaching job is. You might think school districts hire teachers for the upcoming school year in June, but that certainly has not been our experience. One factor working against early hiring is administrators are extremely busy in June with graduation, parent questions about grades, and all the various paperwork they have to complete. Once all the loose ends are tied up from the school year, administrators also typically take vacation time in July. Another factor working against early hiring is the current teachers, themselves. Last minute retirements, illnesses, and injuries are part of life, so administrators sometimes aren't notified of a vacant teaching position until later than they'd like. You certainly shouldn't panic if you don't have a job by mid-August. We've both experienced districts hiring teachers the day before school started or even a few days later. It may seem like nothing's happening, but then you'll get an urgent call at 7 a.m. asking you if you can come in that day!

If you are fortunate enough to get hired ahead of time, you'll be in for both an exciting and frustrating time. Chances are, as a new teacher, you'll have to attend some form of orientation before other teachers are required to be present in school. These orientation days are normally conducted by administrators or teacher volunteers who've been versed in district policy. A positive aspect of this time is you'll get a chance to understand the overall philosophy of the district and how administrators will expect you to approach education. You should stay positive during these days, listen with an open mind, and project yourself as cooperative and professional. Orientation days will also give you the opportunity to meet other teachers new to the district, and you may find these fellow novices will become life-long friends. Once your initial introduction to the district is done, it'll be time for the entire faculty and staff to return for in-service days. These in-service days are prior to the students arriving and are designed to welcome teachers back, introduce new staff members, and orient teachers to district and school initiatives for the upcoming year.

It's at this point you'll have a sense of both excitement and frustration. One thing you must be prepared for is the amount of time you'll spend in meetings. You'll probably want to dive right in, meet the members of your department, get your schedule, and take a look at your classroom, but all of those things will have to wait. Our experience has been that the first day begins with a "welcome back" meeting which may include all the teachers of the school or even the entire district. Such meetings are held in auditoriums or large group instruction rooms and are typically delayed by teachers excitedly reuniting with their friends. Once the teachers are quieted down and seated (they're worse than the kids!), then various administrators conduct their presentations. After a lunch break, it'll be more meetings until dismissal time. If you're lucky, you'll get to meet your department head that first day and maybe get invited to lunch with your department.

After the initial welcome back day, you'll most likely attend a faculty meeting with your school principal and vice-principals. You'll be given more specific information on new initiatives and be introduced to the rest of the faculty. The amount of information thrown at you and the number of people you'll meet might seem overwhelming, but chances are every new teacher feels the same way, so try to relax and soak up as much as you can. It's also during this second day of in-service, you'll have a chance to meet with your individual department members and actually get a chance (hopefully, anyway) to see your schedule. Your other department members will most likely be friendly to you, and it's important for you to pay close attention to the group dynamic. Teachers have a wide range of personalities, so some of them may try to take you under their wing right away, while others may be aloof toward the "rookie." As in any group situation, you'll quickly understand how you fit in with the other teachers. You may also find yourself teaching in different schools (we both had that experience when starting out). Besides the demand on your time traveling from school to school, teaching in two different schools also makes it more difficult fitting in with other faculty members, so you should make an extra effort to be outgoing and introduce yourself to people.

In terms of your classes, realize you very well might be assigned a less than desirable schedule. It's unusual for a teacher's schedule to change dramatically from year to year, although that can certainly happen, so someone retiring or leaving the job opens up rare opportunities for veteran teachers to get the retiree's better classes. As an incoming teacher, then, chances are you'll be given at least some classes no one else wants. Unless you're certified in something specific, such as Physics, you might find your schedule quite different from what you'd envisioned. The lesson here is that if you're expecting to discuss Dostoevsky with an Advanced Placement English class, don't let your world fall apart if you find yourself trying to corral an unruly group of ninth-graders right after lunch. You may also find yourself teaching two or three different classes, a difficult task for even the most experienced teacher, so keep cautiously optimistic and realize your first year, in particular, is going to be quite a grind.

Regardless of the number or type of classes you're assigned, do pay careful attention to your lesson plans. If you're a new teacher, we recommend you have more than enough planned for each lesson, perhaps even twice as much as you think you can cover. It's better to be over prepared than finding yourself with an extra twenty minutes before the dismissal bell rings. Besides wasting valuable class time, it's usually not a good idea to let students have that much downtime. Idle hands are the devil's workshop, as they say! That being said, you also want to ensure your instruction is worthwhile. Students can spot "busy work" a mile off and won't take it seriously. It may help if you have a set curriculum to follow, but even a planned curriculum is no guarantee a new teacher won't run through things a little too quickly. The good news, though, is you'll quickly get a sense of pacing and not run into such potential difficulty for long.

A final concern you may have about what it's like as a new teacher is, "Will the kids like me?" Depending on your temperament, this may not be an issue for you at all, but it's reasonable to assume most people want to be liked by others. If it's extremely important to you for others to like you, it's critical you develop a thick skin as a teacher. You might be teaching 180 students a day, so you should assume some of them will take an instant dislike to you. Whether it's how you look, your voice, your mannerisms, or any other reason, there will always be people who dislike you within seconds of meeting you. Realize there's nothing you can do about that and move on. Some peoples' personalities simply clash, and you'll probably find you dislike certain students for whatever reason, as well. Your job isn't to like or be liked, your task is to instruct students in a given subject. Keep a pleasant but professional relationship with all your students and don't make things personal.

What's the typical teaching day like?

Although you probably want to jump right into what happens once the bell rings and first period begins, you should be aware there are a number of things going on well before the first student walks through your door. One of the first things you need to decide is what time you'll arrive at school. It's a good idea to get there a little earlier than required, especially when you're first starting out. There are a number of tasks you'll need to compete every day and should leave a cushion of time in case anything unexpected happens. You must allow time for checking emails and voice mails, unexpected meetings, students dropping by unexpectedly with questions, and a host of other potentialities that can interfere with your preparation time. You should expect those types of interruptions and plan accordingly. You should certainly have a specific lesson plan ready for the day before you walk in the door. And finally, as bizarre as it may sound, it's a good idea to use the restroom right before classes begin. You might find yourself having four classes in a row and no chance to leave your classroom with proper adult supervision.

Once that first day arrives, you'll certainly be excited and probably a little anxious. We've both known thirty-year veteran teachers who couldn't sleep the night before the first day of school, so it's perfectly normal if that describes you. You'll also realize as your first period of students walks in that you're on your own, regardless of how many times they referred to you as being part of a "team." You'll notice from your very first day that the time of day impacts the class dynamic quite a bit, particularly in early-starting high schools. First periods are normally "dead" and harder to get geared up for than later classes. There are exceptions, but we'd wager you'll find yourself being a sort of cheerleader for that first class. The later in the day, though, the more those classes come alive. Before lunch, after lunch, and the last period of the day will most likely be very different from first period. Last period, in particular, can be a real challenge, particularly if you have windows looking out at the buses. There's something about those buses arriving that causes laptops to close, binders to snap, chairs to move, and students to start getting fussy. Don't worry. You'll get a feel for the rhythm of your classes within a few days and find the best ways to adapt.

One thing we recommend for all your classes is for you to stand outside your door and greet students as they enter your room. Doing so serves several purposes. First, it makes it clear you're the authority figure. If you've just graduated college or just happen to look a little young, you may not look all that much older than your students. One of us even had the experience of being mistaken for a student after teaching for several years. Greeting students at your door also sets a positive tone for your class. As sad as it is to say, yours may be the only kind words or smiling face a student encounters during his or her entire day, so be sincere with how you greet students. Finally, being at your door allows you to assess potential problems either entering your room or developing in the hallway. Fights tend to happen in cafeterias and in hallways, so teachers being alert in the hallways may very well head off trouble before it begins. Sadly, you'll most likely run into such a situation at some point, but you should also be aware you're responsible for less serious issues, too, such as dress code violations (e.g., shirts referencing alcohol, drugs, or targeting a specific group). You're not looking to nit-pick students, obviously, but serious violations must be addressed. Familiarizing yourself with the code of student conduct ahead of time, then, is another important task you shouldn't neglect. If you're ever in doubt as to what constitutes a "serious" violation of student conduct, ask your department head or an administrator.

What else should I expect during the day?

Unless you have six classes or lab classes, you should expect to get some kind of extra duty during the day. Duties take a variety of forms but normally include things like supervising the cafeteria, hallway duty, monitoring a study hall or in-school suspension, or covering classes for other teachers who don't have a substitute. Duties are typically pretty cut and dry; show up on time and do what you're supposed to do. You should be alert on a duty, particularly if you're assigned to the cafeteria. As noted above, cafeterias are prime spots for fights, so it's best to walk around so you're visible to students and look out for potential trouble. If a fight does break out, do *not* try to break it up, yourself. Besides putting you in physical danger, it opens you up to liability if a student gets hurt, even if you're not the one who caused the injury. High school fights, in particular, can get very nasty (such as the time one of us saw a student throw another through the window of the main office), so it's better to do what you can to protect students without getting physically involved.

Another "duty" you may find yourself with is learning the school's technology. You're expected to bring a variety of secretarial skills and a decent familiarity with computer programs when you enter teaching.

Hopefully, you'll receive formal training on the district's grading system and any website that communicates with students and parents, but you shouldn't count on that. Chances are, you'll have to pick up bits and pieces of "how to" information from other teachers as you go along, which adds time and trouble to your day.

In addition to regular duties, you should also expect regular safety drills, such as fire drills, active shooter/lockdown drills, severe weather drills, and evacuation drills. These sorts of drills are part of school life, unfortunately, and you should certainly take them seriously without causing undo alarm to students. Lockdown drills, in particular, are part of modern school life. Explain to students that the chances of a school shooting are small but that it's prudent to be prepared. Stress to them the importance of following procedures and that law enforcement agencies will be involved in some of the drills. Lockdown drills occur even when there isn't an active shooter in the school, so it's important students understand that these drills are for their own protection. For example, one of our schools was locked down because a bank robber was in the area, while another time it was locked down because there was a drive-by shooting outside the school. It shouldn't take such dramatic examples to convince teachers lockdown procedures should be followed *to the letter*. You should also certainly bring up any questions or concerns you have about the drills. Unfortunately, there're a number of ways teachers fail to comply with directives. Common mistakes teachers make during lockdown drills include not locking the classroom door, not moving students away from the line of sight of the door, opening the door when someone knocks (law enforcement officers or administrators will have a key), and not keeping the students as quiet as possible. One teacher even kept his door open a and continued teaching!

How should you handle classroom management?

Another key piece of any teacher's experience is the area of classroom management. How to properly manage student behavior in your classes will go a long way in determining whether you have a pleasant experience teaching or if you burn out and quit. It may sound harsh putting it in those terms, but we've both seen many good teachers get out of education because they couldn't handle the behavior of certain students. Classroom management is part of every teacher's day, so you should certainly think about your philosophy of keeping a class focused on the lesson. Students will test you and see what they can get away with, so it makes sense to be prepared ahead of time. You'll tailor procedures and rules in your own classroom to suit your individual style, or course, but it's a good idea to keep some general ideas in mind. Certainly, any rules for your classroom should be clear, reasonable, and in keeping with your school's code of student conduct.

One of the things we'd suggest is that you put students into assigned seats. Assigning seats has several clear advantages to simply allowing students to decide for themselves where they'll sit. One advantage of assigned seats is you can make seating charts up ahead of time, thus saving class time and cutting down on the stress and activity of the first day of class. Besides helping to organize the class quickly, assigned seating also decreases the chance disruptive students will congregate in the back of the classroom or with their friends. You will also decrease the likelihood of future arguments if it becomes necessary to move disruptive students away from each other. Your seating charts aren't carved in stone, of course, since you may place a student who can't hear or see very well in the back of the classroom, but assigned seating really can avoid some potential problems.

Despite your best efforts to avoid student misbehavior before it begins, there's no doubt the issue will come up. Student misbehavior is a reality of teaching, so it's critical not to make things personal. Some students enjoy making a teacher angry or upset, so it's important you keep cool during times of stress. The most effective way of staying calm is focusing on the actual problem *behavior*. You're not engaging in some kind of power struggle with a student, as much as it might feel that way, but with a behavior that isn't conforming to the classroom or school rules. The best approach is reminding the student what the appropriate behavior is and moving on. You should also make distinctions between childish behavior that can be overlooked and more serious infractions. For example, someone passing gas or a bee flying around in the room might very well disrupt your class. When these types of silly distractions occur, it's best to simply redirect the students to the task at hand and not turn the situation into something serious. The more you react to such things, the greater the chance the situation will become a major disruption as opposed to a minor distraction.

If the misbehavior is more a case of open defiance, though, that's a different situation and must be addressed. Defiance can be either active or passive. Active resistance includes things like a student threatening you, swearing at you, jeopardizing the education or safety of another student, or violating a significant school rule. Such violations of proper student conduct must be dealt with swiftly and directly. Passive resistance refers to students refusing to obey classroom expectations or teacher directions without being directly confrontational. Passive resistance normally takes the form of a student refusing to make eye contact with you and simply ignoring you. You may ask a student to move his seat, for example, and he doesn't do it despite being directed to several times. Although seemingly not as serious as active defiance, passive resistance is definitely a direct challenge to your authority and must be addressed.

We recommend you handle disciplinary infractions yourself as much as possible and avoid involvement of an administrator. Doing so sends a clear message to both students and your principal that you're the person in charge of the room. Sending too many students to someone else for discipline undermines your authority to some extent and draws unwanted negative attention from the administration. At the very least, you should attempt to contact the student's home, explain the situation, and ask for specific ways the parent can support your efforts in the classroom. As always, keep the focus on the student and the fact that certain behaviors interfere with the learning process. If you do find it necessary to refer a student's misbehavior to an administrator, make sure you describe specific *behaviors* in your disciplinary referral. An administrator can't respond very well to a nonspecific description, such as, "The student was disrespectful." Describe what the student actually said or did, not your interpretation of the misbehavior, despite how ticked off you might be. You should also note any conversation you had with the parent and how that conversation didn't lead to a change in the student's behavior.

Given the myriad situations that can arise in your classroom, we didn't think it would be helpful giving you overly specific classroom management strategies. Your education courses should've given you some strategies for handling student misbehavior, and you can certainly find a plethora of information on the topic online. We would suggest, though, you seek out teachers at your school, probably those in your department, and simply ask how they handle student misbehavior. Other teachers can be an invaluable resource for you in this area. You don't have to copy their exact approach to classroom management, but realize veteran teachers are more familiar with the culture of the school than you and most likely have an approach that's at least functional. You may also find a veteran teacher even knows specific students and can save you quite a bit of trial and error dealing with them. Ideally, every adult in the building should be working together to create a safe and effective learning environment, so don't be shy about asking for help.

A note on professionalism

A final topic you should consider is the best way to present yourself as a professional. You've most likely heard to dress and act "professionally," but what does that mean, exactly? Mostly everyone can identify unprofessional behavior when they see it, but it's wise to give the idea of professionalism some thought, since it's a little deeper than you might think. Dressing professionally, for example, is not just about you. Keep in mind that how you present yourself, in part, is a representation of both the school district and the parents. You should dress each day as if you were meeting with a parent or a school board member. Although some teachers dress in t-shirts and jeans every day out of necessity (e.g., if you're an art teacher or dealing with clay), such attire isn't appropriate for most teachers. Since you'll be on your feet most of the day, it isn't necessary to wear high heels or expensive dress shoes, but you should present yourself as someone who takes the job seriously. Beyond that, though, you want to dress in such a way that represents a separation from the students. If you're rather close in age to the students you'll be teaching, it's even more important to make it clear you are not one of their peers, but an adult.

Another aspect of professionalism is how you present yourself on social media. These days, it's almost unavoidable having some sort of social media profile, so it's going to be an issue for all teachers. It should be obvious, but make sure your privacy settings are up to date on any social media you use and be mindful of what you post. Photos or videos of you intoxicated, in sexualized settings, or doing anything illegal shouldn't exist or should at least be deleted as soon as possible. Go back and view your public profile as if you were a parent of a prospective student or as if you were a potential employer. We all say and do things we regret in life, but it's important you minimize any record of improper speech or behavior. It's also wise to be careful with any posts of a political nature. Your job as a teacher is not at all a political one, quite the contrary, so don't cost yourself a potential job by being too vitriolic about your political beliefs.

You should also be aware some students will take a real interest in finding you online and digging into what you've said and done. Students may also film or photograph you in your class when you're unaware of it, so it's a good idea to keep that in mind, as well. You shouldn't be paranoid about your situation, but in a sense, you might very well be under surveillance when you're not aware of it. Part of being a professional is you presenting yourself in a way that would not cause embarrassment if it were played back via video at a later time. Finally, it's also a good idea for you not to involve yourself with students on any non-school-sponsored social media. There are times when coaches or sponsors need to communicate with students via text, but any such communications should be done through accounts monitored by your administration.

Another crucial aspect of being a professional is how you relate to and communicate with parents. You'll interact with a great variety of personalities when dealing with parents, from the supportive to the infuriating, but it's important to treat all parents with respect, patience, and honesty. We've found being as transparent as possible with parents is the best approach. Parents will have questions at times, and you should always be prepared to explain what you're covering in class and why the material is important. In these politically charged times, in particular, you must have proper justification for any materials or information you're presenting to students and how what you cover in class is in keeping with both your school's curriculum and the educational standards of your state.

A final element of being a true professional, and the one most difficult to maneuver, is your relationship and interactions with students. You'll be seeing your students every day and will come to know some of them quite well, but there's always a fine line between being there for your students while not get overly familiar with them. Students may unexpectedly reveal some unsolicited and startlingly personal information about themselves or their families, so you must always be aware of both your responsibility to the student and your responsibilities as a representative of your school district. Students should feel comfortable coming to you as a thoughtful and caring adult in their lives, but you shouldn't do or say anything that would jeopardize the safety of the child or might be interpreted as usurping the role or rights of the parent. For example, you wouldn't feel comfortable giving a student advice about the intricacies of that student's dating relationship and should certainly never do so. Some subjects are simply too personal to discuss. A good rule of thumb is if you wouldn't say something to a student with his or her parents sitting right there, then don't say it if you're having a conversation with the student. An obvious exception would be any discussion of child abuse, as discussed earlier. If a student reports child abuse, you must report it to authorities, regardless of how many times a student might beg you to stay silent.

Concluding thoughts

Despite all the demands you'll have on you throughout your day and all the little things you have to keep track of, always keep in mind you're there for the kids. It's easy to get swept up in the speed and activity of the day, but the ultimate reason your there is to teach, which means your relationships with your students are paramount. The best advice is to be you. Kids can spot a phony a mile off and will immediately pick up on it if you're trying to be someone you're not. If you have a sense of humor, for example, don't be afraid to let it show in your classroom when appropriate. The last thing you'd want is to walk around affecting some dour persona that isn't you. You must be genuine with students, just as you'd be genuine with other teachers, administrators, and parents. It's also okay to be human. For example, talking briefly at times about your life (e.g., places you've traveled, your hobbies, etc.) is perfectly appropriate and can help build a sense of relationship and trust with students. Students should have a sense you're an actual human being and not some automaton that only comes to life when the lights are flipped on Monday morning. Finally, remember you're there for the students. If a student takes the time and effort to seek you out and talk to you, it must be something the student considers important, regardless of how harried or distracted you feel. Put your phone away, close your computer, and give that student your undivided attention for a few minutes. It's what education professionals do.

Chapter 4

THE STUDENTS

Introduction

Regardless of where you wind up teaching, the most important people you'll deal with on a day-to-day basis are, of course, the students. Although it's impossible to say anything specific about students you haven't met, rest assured you'll teach a tremendous variety of students regardless of where you end up. What sort of variety? It could be some of your students will have children of their own. You may teach freshman who look like they're ten-year-olds or seniors who look old enough to have a mortgage. You may have students who've been passed along without developing the proper skills. Some high school students may not even be able to read. You may teach children new to this country who don't speak the language. You may teach geniuses who blow you away with how quickly they master the material you're teaching. You simply can't judge ahead of time the individuals who'll be sitting in those seats. One of the thrills of teaching is you'll also be interacting with hundreds of people a day, each of whom is unique. Although it's impossible to know what will happen in your individual classroom, it's still possible for you to have some sense of what's to come.

A good place to start, once again, is to keep in mind the concept of realistic expectations. The last thing you want to do is approach your job like some sort of jaded cynic (sadly, there are teachers like that), but you should also prepare yourself for a variety of experiences, some of them unpleasant. A critical thing to understand about your students is that they're going to be unpredictable. You may form ideas about the kind of students you'll encounter based on the district that hires you, and other teachers may try to give you their conclusions about students at the school, that's natural. Our advice is to go into your classroom with an open mind, though, regardless of the reputation of the district, and don't let other people's opinions or your own preconceived notions color your interactions or academic evaluation of your students. A short example should illustrate this point.

There was once a tenth-grade class of thirty-five students, only three of whom eventually graduated. They were a very nice, positive group of kids, the kind of students you look forward to teaching. In other words, they were "good" kids. Their grades on assignments and tests were generally decent, but half of the class failed both semesters. What was the culprit? Unfortunately, it was poor attendance. The vast majority of students who failed the class missed almost half the classes or more. Truancy was a school-wide problem, and the counselors and administrators were simply overwhelmed by the number of students who weren't coming to school. When the students were actually in class, they did the work and cooperated nicely, but they simply weren't able to make up for so much lost time. This is just one example of how even "good" kids can fail academically, so realize there're a number of moving parts when dealing with students. The lesson here is you should go into teaching with the idea of being flexible, adaptable, and able to respond positively to different personalities and situations.

Students: The Good

One of the assumptions we do encourage you to make about your students is that most of them will be "good." By "good," we mean most of the students you'll teach will at least be reasonably cooperative, responsive, and willing to engage their studies on some level. Teenagers, in particular, aren't necessarily known for their politeness or emotional stability, and they'll certainly try your patience, but none of those things makes them "bad." Everyone has a bad day, and teenagers have a number of challenges facing them every day, including socially, psychologically, and hormonally. They may curse you and storm out of the classroom on Monday and stroll into your class on Tuesday as if nothing was ever amiss. Or you may have a terrible class on Wednesday, fume about it all Wednesday night, come into class loaded for bear the next day, and find the students behaving like little angels. In fact, we'd be surprised if you didn't run into these sorts of situations. Such will be your lot when dealing with children. Try to remember what it was like for you and how it can be extremely difficult for young people to make it through a school day without having a mini-breakdown. Please be forgiving of them and realize that, at least most days, the majority of them should fall under what you consider "good kids."

And when it comes to the "good" kids, we're also including the quiet students who simply go about their day, perhaps only rarely interacting with you, and then, only when prompted. They may not come off as the warmest of people, but realize students normally have a ton of things going through their minds. They may be shy, worried about their math test, distracted by an argument with a parent, wondering if that pimple is *ever* going to go away, or any number of things that have absolutely nothing to do with you or your class. You certainly shouldn't take such seeming indifference personally. Other quiet kids might see you as their favorite teacher and take delight in coming to your class every day. In their minds, you and they have an important relationship. Take a minute and think about the teachers who've meant the most to you in your life. Are you thinking, at least on some level, about the relationship you had with them? How much time did you spend interacting with those teachers one-on-one compared to how much they meant (and mean) to you? Especially if you were one of those quiet kids, we're betting most of that relationship was based not on actual conversation but on what that teacher said or did on any given day. You'll never know how many of those "quiet" kids will have lifelong memories of you. As with all your students, assume they're the "good" kids until they prove otherwise.

Although it may sound like a contradiction, some of these quiet students will also certainly stand out in your memory. One such student was from China and had only been in the United States for a couple of years. She spoke English very well, but at times had to look up words in her English–Chinese dictionary. She never asked for a clarification of words, even though that would've been perfectly acceptable, and she turned out to be one of the highest achieving students in the class. She was a definite standout in terms of being a model student, but also keep in mind these quiet and studious types may also include students who do what they're supposed to do even though other kids around them are trying their best to distract them. These types of students may not stand out academically in a dramatic way, but they take their studies seriously and go about their business day in and day out. You may never notice such students and how they avoid various distracting temptations, but they'll be in your room and definitely fall under the category of "good" kids.

On the opposite end of the spectrum from the quiet students are the outgoing ones. These are the students who set a positive tone for the entire class. Their positivity and energy are infectious. They're the first ones to answer a question, volunteer for an activity, or be a group leader for their fellow students. One such student took it upon herself to be a sort of big sister to all incoming freshman in the school. She asked them how they were doing, made sure they had a place to eat at lunchtime, and even directed them to their classes. She was a role model and leader for the other students in her grade. We're guessing a number of people in the school were sorry to see her go when her father's job made it necessary for her to move to a new state, but she affected the lives of more people than she knew.

Another outgoing student was a ninth grader who always had a kind word for everyone with whom he came into contact. Normally, ninth graders are a little shy when they first get to a high school, but this student seemed to fit right in immediately. He never had a down day and cheered up his fellow students and teachers on a daily basis. One of his classmates actually got frustrated with his cheerfulness and asked in an exasperated tone, "Why is it you're always so nice?" He responded with, "I just like to bring a little sunshine into everyone's day." The girl shrugged her shoulders and seemed thoroughly satisfied with the answer. These sorts of outgoing students will definitely bring a smile to your face and make you glad you're a teacher, so try to remember them whenever you're having a bad day.

Besides the "average" students, the quiet students, and the outgoing ones, we also include the lovable goofballs with the "good" kids. These folks aren't the greatest of students, necessarily, may frequently grate on your nerves, and get a little disruptive every now and then, but they'll also make you laugh as you shake your head at their antics. Some of these students desperately want to be the center of attention, have issues with concentration, or simply enjoy the lighter moments of life. If you get five or six of these types in a class of thirty-six students, it can get too rip-roaring to teach, so hopefully you'll get them in small doses. They aren't at all "bad" kids, however trying they can be, and you might actually be thankful for them if you're not having the best of days.

One pair of these lovable goofball types stand out, in particular. They were as unlikely a pair as you could ever imagine but somehow became fast friends. One of them grew up in the inner city, was reasonably popular, but certainly didn't get very good grades. The other was a Vietnamese immigrant who had been in the country for only a few years and may or may not have had any other friends in the school. These two sat next to each other in class, and the Vietnamese student took delight in mocking the bad grades the American kid got. One of his favorite expressions was, "You don't study!" followed by both of them laughing together. Not to be out-done, the American student responded by teaching his friend some English vocabulary, the most memorable of which was when the class was taking a final exam. The class was very quiet and then the Vietnamese student said slowly and distinctly, "Aw, f—." Even though it was entirely inappropriate, the entire class erupted into laughter, including the teacher. Needless to say, the language wasn't repeated, but it did give a moment of levity to the class and a lasting memory that still makes me shake my head and smile.

These lovable goofballs, of course, can sometimes go too far, much to their own detriment. One student, in particular, comes to mind. He was one of those students who never stopped talking and cracking jokes. He wasn't a nasty kid or anything, but his daily purpose in life was to get a laugh and be the center of attention. His mother was well aware of his behavior and decided to make a visit to the class. The classroom had a half wall separating the lecture area from the lab area, and this young man's mother decided to come in one day, stand behind the half wall, and just listen in on his usual classroom comedy routine. As usual, he didn't disappoint, talking nonstop and cracking jokes. At one point, he said, "There's somebody back there, and they're throwing up gang signs!" A number of students got a chuckle out of that until his mom stepped around the corner of the wall. All of a sudden, it was tomb-silent except for one student who whispered audibly, "Dude, that's your mom!" Needless to say, this lovable goofball took it too far and interfered with both his education and the education of others. Our hope is he outgrew that immaturity and took school more seriously, but we never saw it. You shouldn't look at students such as him as bad, but as immature and lacking inner discipline.

Students: The Bad

Right away, you may recoil at the very thought of calling any child "bad," but you must realize there's a very small minority of bad actors in the world. It's not the case that every child is an angel, and at age thirteen, a switch is flipped in some of them causing them to turn into little devils. Whether due to genetics, environment, or a combination thereof, it's a sad fact some students will grow up to be dangers to society. How do we define "bad," more specifically? "Bad" kids are the ones who lead a lifestyle of violence against others. They are the predators. As terrible as it may sound, some students are in school to prey upon other kids. That may sound like a melodramatic statement, but if you ever run across someone who fits this description, you'll find our description accurate. These are the students who are remorseless, master manipulators, and will someday be the career criminals who have a dozen felony convictions for serious crimes (e.g., multiple murders, rapes, etc.). These are the people who have no regard for the well-being of others and seemingly take delight in harassing, bullying, and physically hurting others. Make no mistake, though, we aren't talking about kids who get caught up in the wrong situation or with the wrong people and make some mistakes. We're also not talking about crimes of passion, but about cold, calculated actions. We want to stress again that such "bad" students are in a distinct minority, thankfully, but they do exist and you may find one of them in your classroom.

What might some of these kids look like?

A couple short examples should illustrate what we mean by "bad." One was a middle school student who was very funny and outgoing. He certainly had his behavioral issues and clashed with teachers and administrators a good bit, but overall, he was extremely likable, even though he could test a teacher's patience quite a bit. He certainly never showed any signs of aggressive or violent behavior. When he was sixteen, he stabbed his grandmother to death because she wouldn't let him use her car. He didn't show any remorse for what he'd done and said it was her fault because she had been stubborn. Any sixteen-year-old who would kill his own grandmother and then simply shrug it off certainly is someone who is a danger to others.

Another "student" is an even worse example. He was at a party and apparently decided he wanted to kill someone. He called another boy and asked that boy to meet him in order to make a drug deal. When the boy he'd called drove up, this person opened fire immediately and killed him. After killing the other boy, he went back to the party and bragged about the murder. His case went to trial, but he was acquitted of premeditated murder and walked away free. As he was leaving the courtroom, he smiled and winked at the grieving mother. Soon after, this same person was hanging out at the bus stop where the younger brother of the dead boy had to wait for his bus to go home. Mercifully, he didn't harm the younger boy, but the younger boy's mother was absolutely beside herself with worry. This remorseless individual eventually went to prison for premeditated murder, and it's rumored he'd murdered others, as well, though that was never proven. He showed no remorse whatsoever for his actions, and certainly seemed to enjoy them.

Will I have "bad" students in my class?

Thankfully, the chances of you having such a remorseless killer as described above are extremely low. How do we know that? Although you can't make any specific predictions about your students, we've heard from different sources that, regardless of the culture, 6 percent of the population commits approximately 50 percent of the crime. It's a sad fact of life that if you teach for thirty-five years, the chances of you running into someone who will someday run afoul of the law are pretty good, and that person may even spend time in prison. After all, you'll probably interact with around 5,000 young people or more during your time as a teacher, not all of whom are model citizens. Being in a so-called "better" school won't guarantee everyone will be wonderful, law-abiding citizens, either. Some people are very good at manipulating others and can hide their true intentions quite well. You don't want to view all your students as potential criminals, certainly, and you don't want to look at any child as irredeemable, but you also don't want to go into teaching completely naïve. You certainly shouldn't be paranoid about it, but you also must have it in the back of your mind that it's possible you'll be teaching such an individual.

We would caution you strongly, though, not to jump to inappropriate conclusions based on statistics, a mistake many people make. You cannot, for example, assume 6 percent of your students will go on to a life of crime simply because that's true of society at large. The sample size of people you'll be dealing with is far too small to represent all, or even most of society. Drawing such a conclusion about your students is entirely inappropriate from a statistical standpoint. We'd be shocked if all of the students you'll ever teach taken in total would come even close to representing everyone in this country, so be extremely cautious when drawing conclusions from any statistic. You may find you go through a 40-year career and never run across one of the "bad" kids, so take heart and hope for the best.

If I do have a "bad" student in my class, how should I handle it?

Hopefully, your school will have other professionals who can deal with such challenging cases, and you should certainly do everything in your power to aid those professionals. School psychologists, guidance counselors, parole officers, and administrators can be wonderful resources, and you shouldn't be shy about asking for help or advice when dealing with a student. You must also be realistic about your limitations and how much you can actually affect the life of someone who fits the description of "bad." You may think you're the person who can "save" someone like that, and maybe you are, but we would also remind you of your obligation to the other students. It may be very tempting to leave the other ninety-nine sheep to rescue the one lost sheep, but keep in mind you have limited resources in terms of time and energy. We're not saying to ever give up on a student but realize some people are master manipulators and may take advantage of your kind nature and desire to help. The foremost thing in your mind should be the safety and well-being of all students, so don't be shy about involving other adults in challenging situations.

What about the students who're in between "good" and "bad?"

As you probably expected, students don't fit neatly into simplified categories, and you'll probably run into some students who aren't exactly "good" or "bad." A former colleague of ours dubbed certain students "dedicated disrupters," and that label fits as well as any. These are the students who do everything in their power to prevent learning in a classroom, challenge rules, and create as much negativity as possible. They may bully other students, physically threaten other students or adults, and may actually assault adults in the building. They may verbal abuse you every day with no repercussions from parents or administrators, and seemingly delight in aggravating adults as much as possible. Their behavior goes beyond childish defiance but doesn't quite rise to the level of a "bad" kid. These students are not the predatory types who will most likely spend time in prison, but they'll definitely take up an inordinate amount of your time and can put you under extreme stress.

Such students may also take on the form of passive-aggressive types who won't confront you so directly but will certainly challenge you as much as they can and push the envelope in the classroom. They can create a hostile learning environment for the other students by muttering under their breath about any activity or assignment and making it quite clear they don't care and won't try, or do so by their actions. We've both seen students, for example, glance at a standardized state test, toss it on the floor, and then put their head down on their desk. It doesn't matter that they need to pass such a test, they simply refuse to even try. For whatever reason, they don't value education and try to convert others to their way of thinking. They can make it seem like the entire class is against you and lower the standard of behavior for everyone.

Regardless of how these students present themselves, the best thing you can do is remain calm and dispassionate and address specific noncompliant behavior as much as you can. As with any classroom management situation, you don't want to turn it into anything personal or some kind of power struggle, regardless of how desperately the student wants to make it just that. You're the adult, so realize a chronically misbehaving child may be acting out because of a terrible environment or a series of very bad days. As with all students, never give up on these students and hope they'll grow out of this chapter of their lives.

Students: The Ugly

The final type of student we'd like to highlight is the so-called "ugly." By "ugly," we don't mean the students, themselves, but the situations in which they find themselves. Whether they are the victims of physical or emotional abuse, homeless, coping with a psychological disorder, dealing with chemical dependency, or living with the results of poor choices they made when they were younger or poor choices someone else made for them, some children just start out in life with an enormous uphill battle. These are the children who have far more serious problems than doing well in school. What makes it worse is they may come across as extremely unlikable. If you ever get the full story of what they're living with, though, your heart breaks for them. No child should be in their situation, and if you keep in mind some kids are just dealing with more than any child should ever have to deal with, hopefully it will give you a greater sense of forbearance and sympathy when dealing with them. Finally, realize that "ugly" comes in all shapes and sizes and can apply to kids who seem to have everything together. Don't be fooled if you work in a wealthier district, either. Wealth has nothing to do with it. Keep in mind that even if you're the most caring and concerned teacher out there, you probably won't have any idea at all about the hell some of your students are going through, regardless of the type of district in which you find yourself.

Examples abound of how children are victims of circumstances and have been failed by adults in some way. One of us taught a tenth-grade student who literally couldn't sign his own name. Despite passing up the grades since kindergarten, he was illiterate. We've also known kids who were living in cars for various reasons. Some of our students were also taking care of younger brothers and sisters because mom was a drug addict and either missing or passed out on the couch most of the time. We've also taught in schools where students would be beaten up if they got good grades or were seen carrying a book. There are even kids as young as middle school who can get caught up in gangs or criminal activity and find themselves with extensive juvenile records before they even go to high school. Other kids won't even come to school more than a handful of days a year by the time they reach seventh grade.

There are also plenty of kids out there who've made poor choices that set their life on a hard road. One example is a seventeen-year-old in a sophomore class. She had three children by three different men, *zero* credits toward graduation, and had never passed a single class in high school. She was extremely confrontational, nasty, and defiant, and had to be removed from class by security on the occasions when she did show up for class, which was rare. It's clear from her situation she had an overwhelming number of problems in her life, but she was also putting her own children at an incredible disadvantage. It's common knowledge that being raised in such an environment opened her children up to all sorts of pathologies, including poor educational outcomes, substance abuse, and criminality. And the saddest thing of all is that even if she decided she didn't want that kind of life for herself and her children and wanted to turn her life around completely, she'd have an onerous task ahead of her. There was no evidence she ever valued education or that she could even read, so she probably wouldn't be able to read to her children, help them with homework, or give them much guidance making their way through school. There are certainly resources out there to help people in that kind of situation, but it would take a complete restructuring of her mindset to make that help effective. Sadly, the odds are stacked against people in her situation, and against her children.

Although it's easy to see why children such as the young woman mentioned above are in dire straits, other children make such immature and self-harming decisions that it makes you want to bang your head against the wall. The best example we can think of that illustrates such a self-destructive decision involved the wearing of hats, oddly enough. In one school, there was a principal who decided students would no longer be permitted to wear hats. Numerous schools have such a rule, and although some students balk at the idea and carry their hats around like security blankets, putting them on whenever an adult isn't looking, there isn't much pushback about it. Asking students to remove their hats is one of those petty annoyance that teachers across the country deal with on a daily basis and isn't normally an issue that goes nuclear. In this school, though, a dozen seniors felt the no-hat rule was beyond the pale and unacceptable, so they dropped out of high school. They weren't bad kids or anything, but they were just convinced high school wasn't doing them any good, anyway, and that being deprived of their precious hats was apparently the final straw. One wonders what a prospective employer would think about a potential employee who dropped out of high school as a senior over something as trivial as a hat.

What can you do for such kids? Is there any hope for these kids?

As with all your students, our advice in handling the "ugly" situations some students find themselves in is to do the best you can with your limited resources while realizing the obligations you have to the other students. As much as you might be tempted to do so, you can't let your sympathy for one student cause you to neglect your duties to the others. You can't "save" every student, but you certainly can and should notify other adults about any problematic situations your students are facing. We admit we're biased because of the high-quality guidance counselors we've known, but a student's guidance counselor would be the first person we'd turn to. Our assumption is the majority of counselors care quite a bit and would appreciate any information you can give them to help their students. They would also have more direct access to the school psychologist. Another resource you should avail yourself of is your supervising administrator. In cases of suspected child abuse, in particular, remember you're obligated to notify your state Department of Education, but you should certainly also notify your school's administration. Another resource you might consider is the school nurse. Students sometimes feel much more comfortable talking to a nurse about what's going on in their lives than they do a teacher, so once again, don't be shy about seeking another adult's viewpoint or counsel.

So, is there any hope for such kids? The good news is yes. Students may be able to improve their situation with some maturity, hard work, help from others, and some good old-fashioned luck. We'd caution you again, however, about trying to be some kind of savior. We've run into people who have a vision of teachers as earthly angels who sacrifice their lives while being part surrogate parent, part counselor, and part spiritual advisor to hurting children. As acknowledged earlier, such people do exist, but it simply isn't realistic or fair to expect all teachers to be miracle workers. Hopefully, your teaching career will be a long one, and people who expect you to devote every waking moment to teaching simply have no idea of how emotionally draining teaching is. You're one person, with hundreds of people and things calling for your attention every day, so do what you can for your students without burning yourself out in a year or two.

Concluding thoughts

Regardless of how long you teach and how attuned you are to your students, we'd strongly advise you not to judge your students too quickly. You should always keep in mind you may never truly know who's "good," "bad," or "ugly." That ninth grader who keeps pulling his hood over his head may simply be scared and overwhelmed by the size of the school and the number of people there. That same student who, for the first few months of school, says next to nothing may slowly come out of the shell and surprise you with a great personality. The last thing you want to do is make a snap judgment about a student and not allow room for change or growth. How your students interact with you and others can be quite volatile at times, so please keep that in mind as you go into teaching and stay flexible in your thinking. You don't want to get taken advantage of, but you also don't want be afraid to give a kid a second, third, fourth, or 500th chance. Don't give up on your kids!

Chapter 5
THE PARENTS

Introduction

Besides your students, another key group of people you shouldn't overlook are the parents. The importance of parents in their children's lives can hardly be overemphasized. Parents are their child's first teacher (along with siblings), so the environment into which a child is born will clearly impact what goes on later in the classroom. As with your students, the parents you'll encounter come in many varieties and you should guard against forming opinions about them before you interact with them. There are plenty of very good parents out there who have children who don't turn out well for whatever reason so you shouldn't automatically blame the parent for any shortcoming of the child. We've had parents break down in tears at Open House because they were at their wits end about what to do with their child. The child was simply out of control and unmanageable, and the parent had no answers. Conversely, some students turn out amazingly well, despite the horrific environment in which they were raised, so be careful about judging parents based on scant information.

Additionally, realize parents can be yo1ur greatest ally in educating students or they can be the greatest of obstacles. Whether it's Open House, a parent–teacher conference, a phone call, or a chance meeting in a super-market, you're most likely going to interact with parents under different circumstances. Our advice is to keep an open mind when dealing with them and assume they're your ally until they prove otherwise. We often heard other teachers complain about parents, but if the majority of parents were trying to interfere with you, you'd certainly know it. That being said, there are parents out there who don't have their child's best interests in mind or are missing altogether, but thankfully, they're few and far between. Parents clearly are unique, but for simplicity's sake, we're going to address those parents who are "helpful" and those who are "unhelpful."

The helpful parents

By "helpful," we mean parents who, as best they can through their words and actions, send a clear message to their children that education is important and worth pursuing. Even if they weren't the best of students, themselves, these parents do what they can to help move the education process along. They don't necessarily make dramatic speeches about learning, but they do demonstrate education's importance through hundreds of small (and not so small) ways over the years. What things do helpful parents do? One critical thing they do is establish the habit of reading in their children, a skill they'll need throughout their entire lives. Whether it's reading directly to their children, having books around the house, or taking their children to the local public library for story times, these parents make it clear reading helps unlock whole new worlds and experiences. Once the child enters school, helpful parents create a comfortable but serious atmosphere for homework and studying. They ask about assignments and upcoming tests, they familiarize themselves with any online resources the teachers provide, and they keep an eye on grades. If their job allows, such parents also go to parent–teacher conferences and Open Houses. As the student gets older, helpful parents also gradually put more of the responsibility for grades on the students, themselves.

Another important thing helpful parents can do that is often over-looked or left undiscussed is making sure their child is getting enough sleep. We want to emphasize the importance of sleep not only for a child's physical and psychological well-being but also for the critical role sleep plays in a child's education. People are social creatures, particularly as adolescents, and with the constant temptation of social media and games, it's been our experience many of our students were sleep deprived, scarcely able to keep their eyes open during class. If a student is playing video games at 3 a.m. and first period starts at 7:45 a.m. or earlier, that simply isn't enough sleep for the typical student. You should definitely be on the lookout for those sleepy students, and you should certainly alert their parents if it becomes a daily issue.

Finally, we also want to highlight that when we say "helpful," we don't mean "making the teacher's life easier." Helpful parents make a teacher's job easier, certainly, but that's merely a happy byproduct, not the end goal. The true end goal is helping the student gain the most out of the classroom experience. And we make no excuses, nor have tolerance for, the lazy teachers out there. These are the teachers who are teaching the same lessons they did twenty years ago, never bothering to examine if there's a better way of presenting the material to students. They're also the ones who never check to see if the students are actually getting anything out of the material or really learning how to think in the class. These teachers are far too comfortable just doing the minimum and *should* be challenged by parents. Any teacher who feels put out or insulted by a parent asking what's being taught in class and why should be doing something else, truthfully. Parents and teachers should have a collaborative relationship, and sometimes that means parents will have questions. You should be excited to explain what you're doing in class to any parent who takes the time to contact you.

Examples of helpful parents

Sometimes, you might find parents who're obviously your allies. These parents get the message across to their children about the importance of education in no uncertain terms, even if a subject isn't the student's first love. One such parent came in because his daughter was getting a "B" in an Advanced Placement class. Many parents would be happy with that grade, especially given that the student in question was far more interested in subjects like chemistry and physics. Not this parent. He showed up unexpectedly after school one Friday afternoon with his daughter in tow. The three of us then spent the next two hours discussing her preparation for class and how she could improve. This particular father was tough as nails and put the responsibility squarely on his daughter's shoulders. I remember vividly the look on his face as I described what we did in class and the supplemental online resources available to the students. When I had finished, he turned to her and said, "How many hours a night do you study?" She mumbled something around studying for forty-five minutes every day. Within a heartbeat, he blurted out, "You must study more!" He then went on a little bit of a rant to her about how helpful I was being. One line in particular made me chuckle. In an exasperated tone, he told her, "Professor has provided all of this!" I certainly wasn't a professor, to clarify things, but the respect he showed me during the entire meeting was unbelievable. More importantly, he was deadly clear to his daughter about how she had to work harder in the class in order to improve how she studied and how she thought, that it wasn't about the grade. Long story short, she did turn that "B" into an "A" and actually wound up liking the subject matter a lot more. Not every parent meeting, or even most, end in such a happy way, but at least some of them do. Treasure these types of parents who are so concerned about their child learning the subject and improving as a student, and not focused on merely a grade. Your level of concern will never match theirs, but you should certainly do everything in your power to support that parent's message and hard work. They certainly support yours.

There're other times when the helpful parent comes in an unexpected form. You might be pleasantly surprised finding parental allies where you don't expect them. For example, we both had one student who took her studies incredibly seriously and who never even came close to causing a problem in class. One day, her father came into school for some unknown reason to check up on her and make sure she was behaving and doing what she was supposed to do. The gentleman in question rode up on a motorcycle, was a good 6'4", powerfully built, and had the look of a man not to be trifled with. He politely checked on his daughter, who was her usual model self, then hopped on his bike, and drove off. You would never guess just looking at the man that he was such a concerned, supportive parent, but he clearly was. You should appreciate these kinds of parents who're willing to take time from their workday just to check in with you. They're definitely sending a strong message to their children about the importance of their education, but they're also showing you in no uncertain terms that they're standing right there supporting you.

The unhelpful parents

Unfortunately for your students, there're also unhelpful parent out there, as you probably already have gathered. By "unhelpful," we mean parents who, through their words and actions, send a clear message to their children that education isn't of real value. The byproduct of their behavior is that their children have no idea why they're in school and see it as some sort of punishment, which is no recipe for success. Your goals as a teacher come into conflict with the unhelpful parents' goals, so at times, they seem to view you as some kind of adversary to be manipulated or intimidated into doing what they want. As a teacher, your focus is on evaluating a student's knowledge in your subject area and addressing any academic deficiencies. Our assumption is that taking a class is meant to increase students' general knowledge and hopefully help them think in a more sophisticated way. For a teacher, if students leave in June the same people they were in August, something has gone dreadfully wrong. A teacher's focus should be on how can we and the parents can work together to make sure little Bobby gets the most out of his English class even if it really isn't his area of interest and not part of his future career plan. As hard as it is to believe, some of parents work against that very goal of education.

Parents with a misplaced focus

The first type of unhelpful parent we wanted to address is the parents with a misplaced focus when it comes to their child's education. For whatever reason, these parents have taken their eyes away from the final goal of their child being in your class. It's understandable some busy parents get distracted from the bigger picture, but we've found most of them, if they have a few minutes to think about, can see the forest for the trees, as it were. Most parents understand their child's education is an ongoing journey and that they might just experience some bumps along the way. Some parents, though, seem incapable of seeing where their children will be ten or twenty years from now and only focus on what's going on today or this week. These parents may come across as quite concerned but are nevertheless sending the wrong message to their child about the purpose of school.

An example of parents who've lost their way are those parents who are solely focused on the grade their child gets and ignore whether their child is actually learning anything. Their concern seemingly centers around a grade, to the exclusion of anything else. What they want, of course, is the path of least resistance for their child to a high grade. For them, every school before college is simply a means to an end. Given that attitude, you may find such parents even treat you with thinly-veiled contempt and/or condescension. Knowingly or not, these parents are sending the message to their children that school is something to be endured, not embraced or, dare we even say it, enjoyed! When dealing with such parents, or any parents, really, you should always have the details you need to justify why the student has a particular grade. That means your grades should be as up to date as possible and your justification for giving each assignment is solid. Parents certainly deserve full transparency when it comes to their child's grade, but it's especially important when dealing with the unhelpful sort.

One example of a parent whose focus was completely wrong involved a man whose son wound up with an 88 percent for the semester and received a "B." He sent an angry and lengthy email demanding the grade be raised to an "A." After trying to argue that it was, "Only 2 points from an "A," he launched into a tirade about how his son had wasted his time. His argument was his son could've put in far less work, gotten an 80 percent, and still had a "B." He ended his email with, "What lesson are you trying to teach here?" As a teacher, it would be very tempting to put his own question back on him and ask if he was trying to teach his son to do the bare minimum necessary to get by in life, but you should restrain yourself, of course. Instead, it was explained how the grades were calculated and that two percentage points weren't the same thing as two points on an assignment or test. The parent was also gently reminded that education is far more than a letter on a computer screen and that he should take solace in the fact his son took away the most benefit he could from the class.

There are also some misfocused parents who actually hurt their own children by not allowing those children to develop a sense of agency and self-advocacy. A clear example of that phenomenon involved a mother who stormed into a classroom one day yelling about how her son was failing and how it was the teacher's fault. The student in question was a Special Education student, and so this mom believed the teacher was solely responsible for informing her of any missing assignments. It should be noted that missing assignments weren't the reason why this student had a failing grade, but mom chose to focus on this one issue. Not once did she mention anything about her son having to do anything differently, even though he was clearly capable of managing his own assignments. Parents such as these do their children a great disservice because their children never develop a sense of confidence that they can handle situations on their own without outside help. Ironically, it's interesting to note that in this situation the teacher was held to a high level of responsibility for keeping the parent informed than the very parent who was supposed to swoop in at the first sign of trouble. We suppose she qualified as a so-called "helicopter parent," but her own child would've been better off in the long run if she didn't hover quite so close.

Another type of parent with an improper focus is the parent who's angry at their child but wants to take it out on the teacher. Why take it out on you instead of their child? One reason could be they're afraid of conflict with their child or are afraid the child won't listen. A parent may also have had the same conversation with their child two dozen times and simply be at a loss on what to do. Another possible reason you're the focus is that you're an easier target in the parent's mind and are more likely to sit there and take a tongue lashing. They're counting on the conversation not turning into a shouting match, something which may already have happened a number of times in their home. Their assumption is you'll remain calm and will listen, as you certainly should, and so they fire away. These angry parents rarely have a rational argument and meet with you simply to vent their frustration. It's best to just let them blow off a little steam and try your best to determine what's *really* bothering them. Hopefully, you can address an actual issue before their blood pressure gets too high.

It should be noted at this point that although a parent venting is one thing, verbal abuse is something else and should never be tolerated. Verbal abuse can take various forms, but a good rule of thumb is anytime a parent starts using profanity toward you, makes personal comments, or threatens you physically, it crosses the line from professional discussion to abuse. If you ever find yourself in such a situation, just remind the person about why you're there. Something along the lines of, "Mr. So-and-so, we're here to discuss your child's grade, but profanity or personal attacks directed at me aren't helpful. Let's please keep our conversation polite." If such verbal abuse continues, simply remind the parent you're not going to put up with this kind of talk. You can say something along the lines of, "Mr. So-and-so, I've already asked you not to swear at me or use personal attacks against me. If it happens one more time, I'm going to have to end this meeting." If the parent continues despite two warnings, don't be afraid to simply end the meeting. You can just tell the parent you'd be happy to meet with them at another time after they've had a chance to cool down and are willing to discuss matters politely.

More common than the abusive parent is the angry parent who doesn't overstep the line into being abusive but nonetheless makes vague accusations about you being a "bad teacher." Their goal isn't to correct a problem, but to put you on the defensive. As with an abusive parent, try to remain calm and steer the conversation back to the real issue at hand. A simple question like, "What do you feel I could've done better or differently?" may be enough to stop them right in their tracks. You may even find such a question diffuses tension, calms the parent, and leads to a more fruitful dialogue. If you find you did make some sort of mistake, whether in calculating a grade or anything else, assure the parent it wasn't done on purpose and that you'll correct the problem immediately. Once you've taken responsibility for an error and taken steps to correct it, move on and do your best not to repeat that same mistake. If a parent refuses to move forward at that point, all you can do is remind them that the problem has been addressed and that continuing to dwell on it isn't adding anything positive to their child's education.

Parents who struggle to see things as they really are

The second general category of unhelpful parents is the parents who, for whatever reason, have unrealistic views of the teacher or their children, sometimes to the point of delusion. These parents might also be focusing on the wrong issue, but their central problem is they aren't addressing reality directly, potentially much to the detriment of their child. They will most likely push back on you when you try to steer them to what's important for their child's education, but you must, with all delicacy and respect for the parent, try to explain what would best benefit their child from an educational standpoint. All of this may seem vague at the moment, but a few examples should clarify things.

One sad way some parents struggle to see reality is they expect teachers to be superhuman. These are the parents who expect you to be early for work every day, work through every lunch break (which, realistically, may be about twenty minutes), and stay late every day "for the sake of the children." We mentioned in an earlier chapter how some people form an impression of teaching from the movies they've seen but how that impression is completely unrealistic. The movie may show an emotionally-draining scene of a teacher connecting deeply with a trouble class (usually of a dozen or fewer students), but in reality, you'll have five to six classes every day, probably with at least thirty students each. If you think any person can go through an emotionally draining experience with children for forty-five minutes at a clip multiple times a day for years on end, you may want to reassess that expectation. Even if you think we're mistaken and that you are such a person who can handle that kind of stress, you should also keep in mind you have serious obligations to your own family, particularly if you, yourself, have children. If you have a newborn at home and have to go back to work after six weeks, staying late every day simply isn't realistic or desirable. The reality is that if you're planning on having a thirty-five- to forty-year career in teaching, you have to guard against burn out, which is very real. We've both seen dozens of teachers quit after four or five years either because they could make more money in another less stressful job or due to frustration over not being to "save" every child. Trust us, good teachers already go home exhausted every day because they've given it all they have; you can only demand so much from one person.

Other times, parents who don't see things realistically are convinced their child is going to get a full athletic scholarship to college or be a professional athlete. Scholarship money is definitely out there, and no parent can be blamed for wanting all the financial assistance possible, given the exorbitant cost of higher education. Our experience, though, has been that too many of these parents have an unrealistic view of the probability their child will be among the most elite athletes in the country. Besides the low probability of their child getting such a scholarship, there's also the risk of a career-ending injury. Even if a student does wind up with a full athletic scholarship but has focused too much on sports, we also wonder whether that student will have the background knowledge necessary to succeed academically in college. In terms of making to the pros, in our combined fifty-one years of teaching we've only known one student from our entire *schools* who went on to be a professional athlete. The odds are simply against such a thing.

Sadly, we've seen the children of parents who value sports more than academic classes view school as a hoop to be jumped through, and not of any real value. Parents with such a short-term focus on their child getting a college scholarship or making it to the pros don't consider what their child will be capable of *after* an athletic career ends. Even the most successful athletes have to retire, and it's wise to consider what opportunities will truly be available to them. Without a proper education, those options will be limited. Football's Hall of Fame Coach Chuck Noll was fond of reminding his players that there was life after football and that someday they'd be going on with their "life's work." If the opportunity ever arises, you might want to put that idea into some parents' heads.

In addition to the parents who see either you or their children as superhuman are the parents who have difficulty seeing reality because they take everything their child tells them on face value. These are the parents who draw conclusions about you and your class before even talking to you. They see your classroom not through their own eyes, but through the often-distorted eyes of a child. They assume any behavioral or academic issue in class is your fault and will generally look on your motives and your competence with suspicion. They may change their mind about things once presented with facts, but you mustn't count on that. As shocking as it may be, children sometimes try to manipulate their parents and present themselves in a positive light. You can't anticipate every tale that might be spun about your class, but we think we can anticipate a couple of them. Among parents who take their child's word as gospel, a popular view is, "My child would never behave like that!" They find the mere suggestion their little angel would misbehave highly insulting and will immediately turn it back on you in some way. As always, remain calm and keep the focus on the specific problematic behavior the child displayed, trying your best not to get sidetracked. Perhaps the most popular view of all, though, is "My child would never lie to me." Think about that statement for a second. Discretion prevents us from asking, but we'd hazard a guess that some people currently reading this book *still* lie to their mothers from time to time even though they're adults. If you find yourself in such a situation with a parent, avoid using words such as "lie" or "lying," but do make it clear to the parent what the real truth is.

Parents who chase red herrings

If you're ever arguing with someone and they tell you you're bringing up a red herring, what they're saying is you're attempting to draw focus away from the real issue and put it on something irrelevant or insignificant. Parents who bring up red herrings do so, ultimately, because they don't want to contend with a difficult issue or a series of issues involving their child. Sometimes, the issues they focus on are so silly they'd be laughable if it wasn't for the fact their child's education is involved. We've been accused at various times in our careers of being anti-athlete, pro-jock, favoring boys, favoring girls, too conservative, too liberal, and the list goes on. None of those accusations were true, of course, but each of them was meant to distract and put focus on something that had nothing to do with a student's performance in class.

If you come across a discussion centered on a red herring, simply redirect that discussion to the student's progress in your class.

It's been our experience that the most common red herrings concern grades. We've run into several parents who've attempted to bully us into giving their child an "A" because, "He's never gotten below an "A" before." Two things jump to mind immediately. First, how many previous teachers gave in to the pressure and gave the student a higher grade than deserved simply to avoid the inevitable conflict with an administrator (make no mistake, parents like this will go over your head the second they don't get what they want)? You could never say that to a parent, of course. The second thing that comes to mind is what if the situation were a little different, and the student in question never got above a "C" before. Would it be appropriate to tell a parent we were going to give that student a "C," even though a higher grade was merited, simply because it hadn't been done before? No parent would accept such an outrageous justification for a grade. Don't be shocked if you run into such illogical parents, and certainly don't let them bully you into changing a valid grade. In a related way, a parent may switch gears and say something like, "The other teachers are giving 'A's. You're too hard on the kids." This false claim is easily dismissed because you can only deal with matters in your own classroom and can't theorize about what other teachers are or aren't doing in their classrooms. The most critical thing you can do is make sure you can justify every assignment to the student, the parents, and your administrator.

Other red herrings have a more convoluted connection to grades. Perhaps the most childish one is "You don't like my child." Quite frankly, parents who say such a thing are just looking for an easy excuse to justify their child's low grade. Simply reassure any parent who believes such a thing that you're as impartial as possible and evaluate the quality of individual assignments, not how much you like a student. There is an important lesson in this, though. As a teacher, do remember there's absolutely nothing personal about evaluating a student's performance. You may have had teachers who knew you were a good student and simply put an "A" on anything you did without even looking at it, but that's completely wrong and certainly not a practice you should adopt, regardless of how tempting it is to save time. Don't let your personal opinion of a student or the student's previous performances influence how you grade a current academic assessment. Always keep in mind each new assignment or test is unique. Students are smarter than you think, too. We've had several students write something like, "If you're really reading this, draw a smiley face" in the middle of an essay test or paper and were shocked that we caught it. One student commented that he'd been doing such a thing since sixth grade and had never been caught (he was in eleventh grade). It's sad so many teachers didn't bother evaluating him honestly. Always keep in mind that if an assignment is worth giving, it's worth correcting with proper care.

Parents who are missing

The final general category of parents we'd like to highlight are the parents who are missing. The "missing" parents are the ones who're negligent in their responsibilities as a parent, whether they're physically present in the home or not. They may be guilty of neglect, emotional, or physical abuse, or not being in the home at all, but these are the parents who put both the education and well-being of their child in jeopardy. In extreme cases, the word "missing" is far too mild a term for these folks. Dealing with them is more complex than dealing with other parents, but thankfully, they're in the minority. We're going to stress once more that you shouldn't be shy about seeking help from other adults in these tough cases. You can only do so much as one person, so it's always a smart idea to engage other adults who have the ability to help. We've found guidance counselors, in particular, a real godsend when dealing with "missing" parents. A few short examples should illustrate the types of problems you might encounter.

The most obvious kind of "missing" parents are the ones you can't get a hold of or who unexpectedly drop into their child's life. One of the most frustrating experiences you can have is calling a parent and hearing, "The number you are trying to reach is disconnected. No further information is available" or "Voicemail box is full." You may only find out a parent is involved when you get a furious phone call in mid-January demanding to know why the student is failing, despite the unanswered voicemails you left, the ignored emails you sent, and the progress reports mailed from the school. Incidentally, a good place to get a working phone number for the parent is the nurse. The nurse has to talk to someone at home before a student can get an early dismissal or go home sick, so that person typically has the most up to date contact information for parents.

Additionally, some "missing" parents are in the home but are either incapable or unwilling to provide their child with basic care and supervision. Our experience has been that neglectful parents typically have some sort of struggle with substance abuse. Your students may be dealing with a parent who's passed out on the couch every day after an all-night binge of using drugs or alcohol. Children living in that kind of environment may also be caring for a younger brother or sister. A student may be coming in late because he had to drop off younger brothers and sisters at school or leave early because he has to pick up his younger brothers and sisters from school. One student, in particular, comes to mind as a classic case of neglect. His mother struggled so much with alcohol abuse that he wasn't properly toilet trained until sixth grade. Please keep in mind that such situations happen every day and aren't simply dramatic stories. Just like with any circumstance of child abuse, if you suspect a child is being neglected to the point that his physical and mental well-being is threatened, be sure to report it to an administrator.

The most serious kind of "missing" parent, and one we've had limited experience with, are the parents who physically or psychologically abused their own children or have an abusive boyfriend or girlfriend living in the home. Thankfully, neither of us ever had to deal with a victim of physical abuse. Not to our knowledge, anyway. One case of physical abuse that happened at our school was a mother who beat her daughter pretty severely because the mother wanted the daughter's bus pass. A case of psychological abuse that stands out is the one so-called father who was using his daughter as a drug mule. In other words, he was a drug dealer and had his underage daughter transporting drugs for him to different people. The poor girl was eventually arrested in the classroom while she was taking her final exams. We're not sure if she came back to school the next year or transferred, but that was one case of a "father" who clearly had no regard for his daughter's safety, mental well-being, or education. He treated her as a tool to be used to further his own ends.

Concluding thoughts

After hearing some of these stories, you may feel like running and screaming into the night, but once again, take heart. The majority of parents are on your side, but you should keep your expectations about them realistic. By that, we mean you'll probably never meet most of the helpful parents. Just like most of your students, most of the helpful parents will go about their day doing the things they're supposed to do without your knowledge or direction. They may be the people who introduce themselves in passing during an Open House, or they may simply be unknown to you. Sometimes, a few of them will stand out for doing something like sending you a kind email or even a card, but you shouldn't expect such consideration. Parents have busy lives of their own and you are only one of the teachers involved in their child's education. When you're having a bad day, though, try to remind yourself that most of the parents are the helpful sort, doing what they can to help their children succeed and to support you.

Chapter 6

OTHER TEACHERS

Introduction

You may be wondering by this point how you'll find your "voice" as a teacher and what kind of teacher you'll be. By "voice," we mean all the things that make up your individual style and manner of teaching. Your "voice" includes specific things like your rate of speech, speech volume, verbal inflections, hand gestures, facial expressions, use or non-use of humor, and how you move about the room. You won't be directly conscious of all these things, nor should you be, but they all make you unique and will develop and become habit as you go from your first year of teaching on. How do you find that voice, though? Should you try to emulate the best qualities and strategies of teachers you admire or teachers you had as a child? Should you strike out on your own and let your unique teaching style develop organically? Our suggestion is that you do a little of both. It would be silly for you to ignore past experiences, even though your perspective on your own schooling is skewed by the fact you were a student, but it would also be disastrous for you to parrot someone else and lose your own spirit and gifts. What, then, should you do? We recommend looking back on those teachers who most inspired you or taught you the most and use them as a starting point. What lessons can you take from them that fit *your* temperament, personality, and tastes? You also most likely have some knowledge of what not to do as a teacher. Think of the teachers you didn't think were so inspiring or good. What was it about how they taught that strikes you as wrong? How would you do things differently?

In this chapter, we're going to begin by examining effective teachers we had growing up and the lessons we took away from them. You'll notice that even though these teachers had incredibly different styles, what unites them as "good" is that they exhibited qualities that facilitated learning for their students. You may even recognize some of your own teachers in our descriptions. We're also going to look at some former teachers and colleagues who weren't so effective and explain why what they did won't be of service to you in your career. What unites these "bad" teachers is that they, in different ways, interfered with the learning of their students. Our hope is by exposing you to a number of different examples you'll be able to develop some sense of what your own classroom "voice" will sound like.

Helpful lessons from good teachers

It bears repeating that any lesson you teach begins long before you walk into that classroom. You have to conceptualize the lesson, have a rationale for presenting it, prepare for it, and deliver it in such a way that benefits the maximum number of students possible. There are no shortcuts to this process. Students will only see your presentation of the lesson, but they'll easily be able to infer the other aspects of the process. One of my "good" high school teachers showed me the importance of painstaking preparation before class and an organized presentation during class. He came in every day for our Advanced Placement European history class, sat down with his hands behind his head and his feet propped up on the desk, and lectured. There were two things that really struck me about his lectures. The first was that he was an absolute master of content. The details he went into without looking at a single note were mindboggling. His points also flowed naturally and logically from one to another and were presented very clearly. It was evident from his presentation that he had even gone so far as to organize his thoughts into perfect formal outline form, which made our task of note-taking much easier. Although it certainly isn't necessary to have that sort of organization and never even have to look at a note, you should always keep in mind that each lesson requires careful thought and planning. That being said, you should also guard against getting too stuck in your ways. It's important you evaluate your lessons on a continuing basis. Just because you've taught a certain lesson the same way for years doesn't mean you can't find a more effective way to do it. You may also find that a tried-and-true lesson doesn't work well with a certain class. In that case, it's perfectly appropriate and desirable to alter such a lesson. If it becomes necessary to change an ineffective lesson, the more organized you are and the more you know your content, the easier it will be.

It should go without saying, but teachers should be as well-versed as possible in their content. If you presume to take peoples' hard-earned money to teach their children, then you should certainly know what you're about. Why? Because in order to explain something complex in a way that people can understand, you have to truly understand the topic. You can always tell the teachers who don't know their content well because they're the ones who struggle to give a quick summary of what it is they're doing. When you teach, you should be able to start out by giving an understandable overview of the topic before you dive into specifics. I once made the mistake of saying I thought calculus must be impossible to describe in a simple way in front of a calculus teacher. Without missing a beat, he said, "Calculus is the study of continuous change of motion. That'll get you started." What I know about math would fit into a thimble, yet even I understood what he was saying. He clearly knew his subject frontward, backward, and upside down.

Besides pre-class preparation, another critical aspect of teaching is creating the proper classroom environment for learning. This is where being yourself is absolutely essential. Whatever your temperament and personality, it'll come through, so there's no sense in being something you're not. You may be wondering at this point if you can create an environment conducive to learning, but there's no need to worry because there are a variety of ways to create the proper classroom environment successfully. One of my best teachers, in fact, used his unique sense of humor to our advantage. You might've heard the old adage, "Don't smile until Christmas," but that certainly didn't apply to this teacher. He joked around on the first day, made us feel comfortable, but also was organized and focused. His class wasn't easy, but the lesson I took from him was the importance of a warm classroom environment and how important it is to build relationships. He often asked how a student's game went or how the musical was coming along, but not in a time-wasting way. He seemed genuinely interested. He consciously or unconsciously made the class feel like a sort of family, with students getting to know other on a more personal level. His warmth and humor weren't the ultimate goal, obviously, but his style certainly helped him get his points across, got his students to buy into the topic, and made his lessons more memorable.

Another concern of new teachers is usually classroom management, which is another way of saying keeping the focus on why you're there and not on student antics. One of the best ways to avoid potential problems is creating structure and not having a lot of down time. Of all the teachers we had, ourselves, the first one who comes to mind as someone to emulate is a sixth grade math teacher. What struck me about her class was how, from the moment we walked in until the moment we left, we were engaged in some sort of activity. I didn't realize it at the time, but she had an extraordinary organized and efficient system for teaching and was a wonderful classroom manager. She was actually teaching three different levels of math in the same classroom. Her strategy was to teach one section while the other two sections worked on activities. She ran an incredibly tight ship, and no one ever thought of stepping out of line in her class. In fact, I was a little bit afraid of her for the first part of the year. It's funny, looking back on it now, because

I met her years later, and she couldn't have been more than five feet tall and couldn't have weighed more than ninety pounds, but she ruled her classroom completely. The tone of her class wasn't exactly what you would call "cold," but it was certainly professional. She never deviated from talking about math and only rarely smiled. Her style and my style were quite different, but I always remembered the organization of the class and now much math I learned that year because of the environment she so carefully created. Any good teacher should give thought to the type of environment to create in the class, with the ultimate goal being maximizing benefits to the students.

Hopefully, one of the things you gathered from the above teacher is the fact that what you look like has no real bearing on managing a class successfully. You, yourself, may be of rather small stature or look very young and have doubts about whether students will take you seriously, especially if you'll be working in high school. Rest assured, it's all in your preparation and how you conduct yourself. You don't have to be a big man with a big, booming voice to get kids to listen to and engage with you (neither one of us fit that description, certainly). In fact, it was our experience that the best teachers at managing a class were not the drill sergeant types but were calm and only rarely, if ever, raised their voice. What you do have to be is someone who has something worthwhile to teach and a willingness to do so. Be yourself, keep a good focus, make sure your lesson is paced appropriately (i.e., don't waste time and don't leave too much time at the end of the class), and you'll have as much a chance as any other teacher of keeping your class focused. That being said, even the best classroom manager can have a class get a little out of hand, so realize you'll have those kinds of days and look forward to better things tomorrow.

Besides teachers you've had in the past, another good source of information on effective teaching techniques are your fellow teachers. The members of your department, in particular, should be able to answer your questions and give you helpful tips along the way. You may even be assigned a veteran teacher to act as a sort of mentor your first year. Once again, you don't want to simply ape what someone else is doing, but you should also be receptive to different views and approaches. You'll have a lot of trial and error your first year of teaching, in particular, so don't be afraid to ask for guidance or suggestions when you need it. Even after you've been in the game awhile, you'll notice other teachers can be of invaluable service. For example, it'll probably be other teachers who show you how to use new technology. It was our experience that new computer programs were implemented without the staff being properly trained on them. In fact, sometimes we weren't trained at all. In that kind of situation, it'll be you and your fellow teachers putting your heads together to figure things out.

Helpful lessons from bad teachers

Similarly to the parents and students, you'll undoubtedly run into a wide variety of teachers during your career, some of whom are "bad." These are the teachers who, for whatever reason, interfere significantly with the learning process of their students. They aren't malicious or anything, it's just that they've somehow lost sight of their primary function. We've all had bad teachers, ourselves, and can spot a bad one when we see one. Unfortunately, these bad teachers seem to skate by year after year and are just accepted for what they are. Department heads and administrators can certainly work with these teachers to help them improve, but some people simply ignore any kind of suggestions and go along their merry way. The good news, though, is you can certainly learn from bad teachers by not repeating their mistakes.

The first mistake some teachers make is they think yelling at students is an effective classroom management strategy. As much as students will test your patience at times, losing your temper and engaging in an emotional outburst is the wrong move. If you have a habit of doing that, you may quickly find students making a kind of game of it, seeing if they can make you angry because they find your outbursts entertaining. It's also the case students quickly become desensitized to yelling, and it becomes completely ineffective. An experience with a 4th grade teacher illustrates the ineffectiveness of yelling quite well. Her situation was a difficult one, admittedly, because her class was made of third graders on one side of the room and fourth graders on the other. As you can imagine, the level of maturity of the kids wasn't all that great, but this teacher wasn't suited for dealing with younger children. About every other week, she would stand at the front of the class and lecture us about some aspect of our bad behavior. After about ten minutes, she had literally worked herself into tears and was screaming at us. It probably was effective the first time, but there are only so many times you can take such tirades seriously. My most vivid memory of her is her going on one of those long rants, tears streaming down her face. She paused at one point, only to have one of the third graders make a fart noise. When you're in third or fourth grade, nothing brings the house down quite like an expertly timed sound effect, and our entire class erupted in laughter. Let's just say the spell was broken at that point and her yelling had zero effect after that. It's okay to lose your temper at times as a teacher, these things happen, but the lesson here is to avoid making a steady diet of it.

Another way a teacher can be "bad" is by teaching the students at a level either too far below or too far above their ability. You should know what your students are capable of and teach them at an appropriate level. How you do that is by checking for what they already know *before* you teach and checking for how well they understand the material *as* you're teaching it. People tend to focus on unit tests, which is appropriate, but don't neglect keeping your finger on the pulse of the class during the entire course of a unit. You should certainly know you aren't there to rigidly stick to some lesson plan, unit plan, or curriculum at the expense of your students. If it's in the best interest of your students to speed things up or slow things down, by all means do so.

A former eighth grade teacher comes to mind immediately as illustrating this kind of inflexibility and unwillingness to adapt. The original teacher was well-meaning and pleasant teacher, but it was clear to the administration she didn't know her content well enough, and so she was let go after the first semester. Her replacement was a retired teacher who was brought back from mothballs, dusted off, and put back in the classroom after not having been there for something like eight years. This replacement teacher made the mistake of not tailoring her instruction to the student she had. Specifically, she had always taught the younger grades and so began teaching multiplication tables, something every student in the room had already mastered a number of years previously. The students were a cooperative group and didn't complain about getting easy work, but it should have been painfully clear to her that they were far too advanced to simply do single and double-digit multiplication problems all class. What she should've done was assess the class's general knowledge of eighth grade math and then figure out where the weaknesses were. Instead, she simply taught what she was comfortable with and ignored the needs of the students. Some of the students had parents who taught them the appropriate level math, but a far greater number went into ninth grade ill-prepared. Such a situation could've and should've been avoided with just a little forethought and effort. Always remember that a good teacher has a grasp on what the students already know and just how much to challenge them with new material.

Knowing your students' capabilities and being vigilant about assessing their progress on new material, ultimately, is part of being properly prepared for class. A teacher's unpreparedness definitely interferes with the students' education, and so it's something you should always guard against. Even the best teachers sometimes misjudge how long a lesson takes, but what separates the good teachers from the bad is the frequency such things happen and how they respond to it. If you're one of those teachers who come to class chronically unprepared, we strongly suggest you commit yourself to a new work ethic. Look at it this way: if your lack of preparation costs the students 10 minutes of instruction time a day, that's 50 minutes a week, about 200 minutes per month, and about 2,000 minutes per year. In simple terms, your lack of preparation's robbing your students of over thirty-three hours of instruction time, time the parents are paying for. We're not suggesting you constantly watch the clock and squeeze out every last second of class time, but we are suggesting you be mindful of the fact you have an important job which requires your serious attention. One short example should illustrate what we mean.

One teacher typically came to class late and seemed to always be distracted and disorganized. He also needed several minutes to figure out what he was doing, virtually ignoring the students. Luckily for him, he had upper-level classes that were well-behaved, otherwise, he might have never gotten his classes under control due to so much down time. His lack of preparation also got him in hot water more than once. He tended to show a number of video clips during his lessons but never took the time to preview them. There were several instances of profanity popping up in the videos and one incident with full nudity. Besides exposing students to inappropriate material, his behavior sent the message that what they were studying wasn't exactly worth the effort. If the teacher treats the class material in such a cavalier fashion, why should students be expected to take it seriously?

Another lesson you can learn from ill-prepared teachers is not to confuse having a plan as an impediment to creativity. For some teachers, there seems to be a misconception that too much planning kills creativity. It's as if they believe going into class with just vague idea of what they want to do gives them a better chance of being "inspired." The exact opposite is true. Truly creative people, besides being rare, are also quite knowledgeable in their field. As a teacher, you shouldn't go into a class and expect a lightning bolt of inspiration to hit you. It may sound counterintuitive, but the more prepared you are and the deeper you know your subject, the easier you'll be able to adapt your lessons. It's been our experience that teachers who aren't ready for class tend to do the same type of lesson over and over again. Unprepared doesn't equal creative.

There's also a real danger that not being ready for class might tempt you to be what we call a time-waster. You don't have to spend every moment talking about school, but make sure what you're talking about is at least in some way relevant. For example, one of us had a teacher who would ask us about our sports teams or even how sick family members were doing. She wasn't wasting time but was demonstrating that she cared and wasn't just some kind of robot there to teach. Other teachers, though, took a different approach, and actually wasted class time. An example of this kind approach was exemplified by a teacher who was a huge baseball fan. Besides being a fan, he'd actually played baseball professionally and was fond of talking about his time in the big league. On virtually any sunny Friday in the spring, all a student had to do was ask, "Mr. So-and-so, didn't you used to play baseball?" to get out of class. As soon as that question was asked, he'd start telling stories about his baseball days and the entire closed the books, knowing the class was over. That strategy also worked around the time of the World Series in the fall. As a teacher, there's nothing wrong with sharing your interests, but it shouldn't get to the point where it interferes with your class. This particular teacher wasted entirely too many class days talking about sports. If half the class is gone on a field trip or out with the flu, then it's perfectly fine to talk about baseball, ballet, the movies, or whatever else holds everyone's interest, but it should happen only rarely, if at all.

Besides wasting time, you should also avoid worrying too much if you're liked by the students. New teachers seem to make this mistake more than veterans, but even teachers who should know better can fall into this trap. For example, one teacher had students who were fond of saying, "I love Miss So-and-so. She's more like a friend than a teacher." We certainly wouldn't take such a statement as a compliment. Most people want to be liked, of course, but keep in mind your job is to teach. If the students like you, that's great, but it's far more important that they respect you. This particular teacher apparently made very few, if any, demands on her students and gave a number of easy A's. It seemed she also had a habit of coming to class five minutes late and running her class as a discussion session. Our experience has been these teachers who want to be liked make either a conscious or unconscious decision to make their classes extremely easy. It's also no coincidence that enrollment in these teachers' classes is usually extremely high. Kids are kids and enjoy getting good grades without working very hard, but that certainly isn't doing them any favors in the long run.

Closely related to the teachers who want so desperately to be liked are the teachers who are inordinately involved in the gossip of the students. They are the ones who are always up on the latest drama of who's dating whom, which couple just broke up, whose parents are getting divorced, and any number of other details a teacher shouldn't be involved in knowing. We've run into teachers whose conversations center around what the kids are doing and nothing else. There are certainly times when you'll talk about what's going on with the kids to other teachers, but it won't be a typical topic of conversation. If you encounter one of these teachers, we would suggest you not involve yourself with the drama and try to either redirect the conversation or tell the person you aren't comfortable discussing such things. Unfortunately, even if you never say a word during one of these conversations, you might get the reputation of someone who talks about the kids simply because you're around somebody else who does. If that concerns you, the best thing to do is simply excuse yourself and walk away when the gossip starts flowing.

It's also the case that some teachers get overly concerned with the gossip surrounding fellow teachers. There was one substitute teacher who fit this description perfectly. His ears perked up at the first hint of gossip, and if anyone walked into the teachers' lounge he would say, "Did you hear about such-and such?" before he even said hello. Just remember that if you engage in such gossip, yourself, you'll quickly get the reputation as someone not to talk to. As one person said about that substitute, "Don't tell him anything unless you want the whole school to know." We strongly suggest you avoid petty gossip like that. It seems people gossip no matter where you are, but you'll have challenges enough as a teacher without having to engage in additional negativity from your peers. As a general rule, too, avoid badmouthing other teachers in front of students and take anything students tell you about another teacher with a grain of salt. One of us was actually put into an awkward situation with another colleague over student gossip. This colleague fired off an angry email saying something to the effect of, "So-and-so said you said this about me." I sought this person out and explained I'd never even mentioned her name in my class and that the student was lying. She accepted that explanation with ill-favor and seemed to stay angry about the non-issue for months. Sadly, even adults are susceptible to the "He said – she said" trap of adolescence.

Other teachers don't get caught up in the trap of gossip but do get caught up in the trap of politics. Unless you've been living in a cave somewhere, you're surely aware of how divisive politics are these days. That divisiveness has certainly found its way into the schools. It seems some people go so far as to see politics as some sort of religious struggle between good and evil. One department head even tried to get a substitute fired because that substitute was of a different political party. Unfortunately, there're teachers out there who've forgotten their primary focus and instead believe they are on some kind of crusade to proselytize students to their political way of thinking.

One such teacher seemingly was attempting to indoctrinate her students into seeing the world through her political lens on a daily basis. What she failed to keep in mind was that she was a representative of both the district and the parents, among whom there were a variety of political opinions. Talking about politics is unavoidable at times, but at no time should your personal views affect presenting different political views from a fair and dispassionate perspective. You should also be aware that since the COVID lockdowns of 2020–2021 and the use of more online learning, more parents are taking an active role in monitoring what their children are being taught in the classroom. We believe you should have no problem with a parent seeing or hearing what you do in class; they pay your salary and you're dealing with their kids. You should certainly not try to hide what you're teaching. When it comes to politics, you may have the best of intentions and only want to present what you consider the "correct" views, but remember that the road to hell is paved with good intentions, as the saying goes. Your job isn't to create classes of brainwashed little party loyalists, regardless of which party or belief system you follow, but to teach kids to think for themselves. It's always best to keep the politicking out of the classroom.

Perhaps the teachers who do the most to damage the reputation of all teachers are the ones who are just plain lazy. It should go without saying that you should learn nothing from such teachers except what *not* to do. These are the teachers who do the bare minimum necessary not to be fired and interfere significantly either with their own job prospects or with the education of their students. Several examples come to mind immediately. The first involves a day-to-day substitute who'd been looking to get hired on full-time for at least two years. He finally had the chance to prove himself when a full-time teacher took a semester off on medical leave. Unfortunately for him, it didn't take long before he demonstrated his work ethic wasn't up for the job. Throughout the semester, he often boasted about how little work he did to anyone who would listen. Two weeks before the semester ended, he even bragged about how all his grades were already done and how he was just showing movies for the final two weeks. What he didn't realize was that word of his antics made its way back to administrators via students and other teachers. Not surprisingly, when it came time to choose a permanent employee, he wasn't even given an interview.

Another example of a lazy teacher involved one who was, quite frankly, counting his days to retirement. He took a sick day every Friday during the year and spent quite a bit of time giving kids worksheets to fill out while he sat behind his desk. When another teacher had to cover his class one day and insisted students do the work they were given, one of them fired back with, "Why do you care? Mr. So-and-so doesn't." The kids weren't stupid, they realized he was just going through the motions in order to collect a paycheck. Another appalling thing he did was sign up for three cafeteria duties in a row so that he had no free time during the day. Why would a teacher ever do such a thing? He was doing it because, in his state, a teacher's pension was based on the highest three years of income. This teacher was obviously trying to pad his final years of retirement so that he would get a larger pension. There's nothing at all wrong with maximizing your pension, but this individual was clearly cheating students out of the education they deserved. Sadly, the administration knew exactly what he was doing but made no effort to stop him. It certainly would've been possible to give this teacher unsatisfactory ratings, but apparently, the administration didn't feel it was necessary to bother with it.

The most brazen example we can think of a lazy teacher involved one who was assigned two separate courses to teach. Having two different courses to teach was typical for us throughout our careers, and certainly wasn't any sort of hardship. This teacher, though, decided he would simply teach both separate courses as if they were the same. He used the same curriculum, the same assignments, and the same tests for both courses. Since the two courses weren't as easily distinguishable from each other as, say, World Cultures and Psychology, he was never caught by an administrator. It was without question an administrator's responsibility to understand what he should've been teaching, but none of them took the time or effort to look at the curriculum for either class, so he got away with it. No teacher should ever have done what he did, obviously, so the blame ultimately rests on him, but it was the students who truly suffered.

The final examples of "bad" teachers we want to highlight are those who create a hostile learning environment for their students. You may think kids need a firm hand, and you might even think they need toughened up a little bit, but there's a difference between being a tough teacher and being abusive. If a student's afraid to come to class every day or is dreading every interaction with you, that's a red flag and a situation that needs to be dealt with immediately. Children put in that kind of situation aren't learning anything but fear, which is very wrong in a school setting. If you ever wonder if you've crossed a line, you need to examine your motives and see if you truly have the child's best interest in mind and if your approach is effective. Not every child is the same, obviously, so there are some who need a gentler hand than others. You may think your treatment of the student is perfectly fine, but you should consider what affect your behavior is having on the student. It could very well be that things can be cleared up with a short parent meeting with the child present, and that's certainly the first route we suggest you take. Your students should respect you, but they shouldn't fear you. Remember that the ultimate goal is to educate the students, not intimidate them into doing what you want. Thankfully, we've run into very few teachers who fit this description and certainly hope you don't see yourself in the above description.

One teacher who did create a hostile environment made a habit of sexually harassing certain female students. If one of them came in with an outfit he liked, he'd have her twirl around to get a better look at her. That sort of degradation and humiliation of students should never be tolerated in any classroom. No student should ever feel in the least way uncomfortable around his or her teacher or have to worry about unwanted attention or touching of a sexual nature. And the same goes for making comments of a sexual nature about a student when the student isn't around. Just because a student doesn't hear such a comment doesn't make it less reprehensible. Unfortunately, we've both run into teachers who've made inappropriate comments about students. Don't simply let such disgusting comments pass unchallenged. You shouldn't feel uncomfortable reminding another adult such comments aren't appropriate when aimed at another adult, much less a child. If confronting such a person isn't your style, you should at least make it clear you aren't comfortable discussing others in that way and remove yourself from the situation immediately.

As an important side note, you must also remember that, regardless of your gender, it's important you guard against even the appearance of impropriety when it comes to children. This can be an exceptionally tricky situation if you're very young-looking or close in age to the students you're teaching. You may find students flirting with you, sometimes shamelessly. You must absolutely, unequivocally shut that sort of thing down. You don't need to get hysterical or anything like that, but just make it very clear it's inappropriate for any student to look at you that way and that it won't be tolerated. You should also be careful when it comes to any sort of touching with students. Even a pat on the shoulder can be misinterpreted by some, so be judicious when it comes to touching your students. You have to judge for yourself based on your personality and the situation, but there's really no necessity for touching a student and we recommend avoiding it entirely. Male teachers, in particular, need to be especially careful.

You should also realize it only takes one unfounded rumor to destroy your reputation, particularly if you're a man. That comment may sound sexist, but we're just basing it on our observations through the years. We found that boys, in general, may brag about their imagined sexual exploits with a female teacher but take it no further. We've both noticed that girls, on the other hand, have tended to make false accusations of sexual harassment or abuse against male teachers. There are certainly teachers out there who prey on children, make no mistake, but there are also those students out there who carelessly ruin a person's entire career by making false accusations. We're assuming sometimes the child is acting out of spite, but we're also assuming the child is unaware of the long-term consequences of making such a serious accusation. Even comments like, "You're my boyfriend/girlfriend" or "I'm taking you to prom" aren't simply innocuous statements to laugh about. You don't want to make a federal case out of them, but do want to make sure they get nipped in the bud.

Concluding thoughts

Although we've focused more on some of the bad teachers, the truth is that there are far more good teachers out there than bad. There are a variety of ways a good teacher can conceptualize, prepare, and execute a lesson, so it would be impossible to examine all of them. A properly prepared teacher, for example, will look different, depending on the class and the grade level being taught. As long as you take your job seriously, give it your best effort, and seek out the advice of others, you should be fine. And don't worry about the process of becoming a teacher. It'll take about five years before you feel completely comfortable teaching a class, so don't be afraid to experiment a bit and truly refine your "voice" as a teacher.

Chapter 7
ADMINISTRATORS

Introduction

The final group of people you'll work with we wanted to highlight are the administrators, your principal, assistant or vice principals, and your superintendent. Besides a wide variety of administrative jobs, it's the administrators who are ultimately responsible for helping maintain order in the school, including the cafeteria, hallways, and yes, even the classrooms. If anything goes dreadfully wrong in the school, it's the administrators who will get involved and be held responsible to some extent. They have an extremely important and stressful job, and you should always respect that. In terms of how they affect teachers, administrators will be the ones evaluating your performance and will hopefully make it possible for you to do your job without being assaulted, harassed, or prevented from teaching by chronic misbehavior.

During our careers, we worked with dozens of administrators and had relationships with them ranging from very friendly to downright adversarial. One incompetent or mean-spirited administrator can make a teacher's life extremely difficult, so you should learn how to work your way around such people as best you can. During our careers, we always said, "It's not the kids who get you, it's everything else." By the end of our careers, unfortunately, a big part of "everything else" was the administrators. In this chapter, we're going to distinguish between administrators and teachers and give you some of our experiences, both positive and negative. You shouldn't draw conclusions about your administrators until you interact with them, of course, but you should also have an idea of how their job differs from your own.

Administrators set the tone for the school

Of all the administrators you'll deal with, the most important is the principal. A principal who doesn't do the job correctly can set a bad tone for the entire school. One example that comes to mind is a principal who was completely over his head. On a personal level, he was a very nice guy, but he lacked the backbone to say something and mean it. During his tenure, it was routine for at least fifty kids to be in the hallways during classes. Besides obvious safety issues, it made it more difficult to teach with all the extra noise and kids periodically opening your door to say hi to one of their friends in your class. It became so absurd that on one memorable afternoon, a group of students who'd left school grounds came walking into the cafeteria wearing Burger King crowns and carrying Burger King bags! It was also quite common for kids to cut school, particularly in May. One teacher had four classes of seniors and didn't even have half of them in class on any given Friday. Other classes weren't much better in terms of attendance, either. Every now and again this administrator would get angry and get on the PA system to talk about rule changes and enforcement, but it completely backfired. Typically, he started off sounding very tough, rambled on for a few minutes, and then backed away from his tough talk, sometimes with comical results. His most memorable line is when he was talking about cracking down on misbehavior and said, "There definitely *may* be consequences." The kids in the class bursting into laughter when he said that. Eventually, this administrator was transferred to a smaller school with younger students and fit in just fine. The principal who replaced him was actually applauded by the staff members during the first faculty meeting. He certainly had his hands full reworking the culture of the school, but he was able to do it. Unfortunately, the new principal was transferred a few years later, and the culture of the school started to slip again. You should never underestimate how much influence a principal has over the culture of the school, and you should be very thankful if you have a good one.

Administrators aren't teachers

An important thing to keep in mind when dealing with administrators is that, although they may have once been in the classroom, they are *not* teachers. We've both seen various people who couldn't hack it as teachers become high level administrators. In fact, one of the most arrogant and self-assured administrators we ever heard of was found crying outside his classroom during his brief tenure as a teacher. There are other administrators who served as guidance counselors and never actually taught in a classroom. Being a successful classroom teacher isn't a prerequisite for being a good administrator, but our point is that teaching and administrating aren't the same job.

Perhaps the confusion over administrators and teachers is perpetuated by the media. When the media talk about education, they often use the generic labels "the school" or "the teachers" to refer to any official policy stance by the school board or administration. Administrators are also often counted as "teachers" for purposes of calculating average class size for a district. Many people, then, seem to make the false conclusion that "the school" and "teachers" are interchangeable terms. It is true teacher surveys may factor into how a school policy is developed or implemented, but the ultimate decision of whether or not to adopt policies is made by administrators. Administrators may also simply announce a new policy to staff members without any foreknowledge of the teachers. It's also the same situation with teachers' unions. Teachers may be union members, but that doesn't at all mean the teachers of the union are in lockstep when it comes to recommendations, actions, or political endorsements.

Administrators have a very tough job, and they often have a thankless job, as well. One of the things we've said consistently through our careers is, "You couldn't pay me to be an administrator." They have to deal with budgets, the superintendent, school board members, the media, irate parents, a variety of student issues, and, of course, teachers. They also may find an inordinate amount of their time taken up by required meetings. They also don't get the satisfaction of teaching a subject they love every day. No one forced them to become administrators, of course, but realize they have many different demands on them, too, just like you will. Our advice is, as much as it's up to you, maintain a pleasant and professional relationship with them. You certainly don't want to fall into the trap of chronically bad-mouthing the administration. Blowing off a little steam is one thing, but some teachers make it such a habit that it creates a negative environment. Besides not doing anything constructive, going into work every day with a bad attitude will make your job even more difficult than it already is.

Administrators have different incentives than teachers

Although your interests and the interests of administrators do coincide at times, you also must be aware that their incentives are different from yours. An example of varying incentives can be seen in how administrators and teachers look at overall student grades. As a teacher, you're interested in individual students and how they're doing in class. If a student isn't doing well academically, you're going to look at specific assignments and see if there's any kind of pattern or any kind of insight into improving the student's achievement. Some administrators, though, are only interested in descriptive statistics and whether or not there's any kind of disparity between or among groups. They show remarkably little concern about discussing individual students and wanted only to focus on how one group of students, on average, stacks up against another. Why? We believe the answer lies at least partially in the fact that it's easier and faster to compare demographic groups than it is to dig down into the data. Some administrators are only interested in *if* different demographic group's grades are different, not *why*. The assumption is that disparities between and among groups are a sign of a problem. Instead of recognizing that disparities between and among groups are the norm, not the exception, they take the easier route and simply put it back on the teacher to explain why one group of students did better on average than another. Frankly, it's a lazy and easy way of avoiding any kind of serious analysis of student performance and progress.

A personal example from one of the authors will illustrate what we mean. One of us has a sibling who's quite similar in temperament to us. We were raised in the same household, went to the same grade school, high school, and college, and had many of the same experiences. Our academic paths branched off into completely different directions, though. While one of us graduated with a degree in History and went on to become a teacher, the other graduated with a degree in Chemical Engineering and had a very successful career in the military. Our grades in science and math classes differed greatly, but the differences were due to the fact that our natural abilities and interests weren't the same. If two siblings raised in the same household and attending the same schools had such disparate outcomes, why would anyone expect large groups of people to choose the same academic course and wind up with the same grades? We should also keep in mind that, statistically speaking, differences *between* groups won't be nearly as pronounced as differences among people *within* those groups, but the point is that very similar people can make very different choices. You should see your students as the individuals they are, and not simply as a set of numbers on a computer screen.

Let's use another example comparing two hypothetical classes. Assume both classes are absolutely identical in terms of demographic groups. One class meets third period and the other meets last period. Would it be reasonable to expect both of these groups to have identical grades? On the surface, you might think yes, but let's examine some other factors that may affect scores. It could be the class at the end of the day is affected by kids leaving early for sporting events or kids leaving early because they're cutting class. It might also be the case the students are more wound up the last period of the day, which is quite typical, because they've been in school a long time and are ready to go home. Or it may simply be the case that a particular group of students just set each other off for no apparent reasons. These are just some of the factors that might impact student grades, and we certainly haven't provided an exhaustive list. It simply isn't appropriate to compare group data without digging deeper into other factors that may have influenced those data. Some administrators, though, have no interest in hearing about any such "excuses" and will automatically conclude any differences in outcome are prima facia evidence of inequitable treatment of students. Their assumption is that if the teacher treated all students "equitably," then there would be absolutely no disparity among test scores or grades between or among groups. Curiously, we've never heard of an administrator ever suggesting how to correct such supposed inequitable treatment, despite the assumed necessity of doing so. In fact, we've never even heard anyone provide a specific definition of "equity." If you'll take our advice, you'll never discuss groups as a whole without delving into the individual students who make up the group. We know from basic statistics that what's true of a group isn't necessarily true for an individual within that group, but you might be surprised how many administrators seem to have never heard that rule or choose to ignore it.

In quite a similar fashion, it's been our experience that administrators tend to look at standardized testing scores differently than teachers. Their focus is once again on group disparities on those tests, while your focus will be much more on individual scores. It may be instructive to compare the achievement of different classes or demographic groups, but ultimately, you're going to have to roll up your sleeves and do some work to come to any meaningful conclusions. The fact that there are differences between or among groups doesn't tell you *why* those differences are there. When you think about it, any kind of test, standardized or other, measures what's happened in the past, but they don't explain what happened or why. Did a student do poorly on a test because of lack of studying? Was that student feeling under the weather the day of the test? Did a student break up with a girlfriend or boyfriend the morning of the test? The point here is that standardized test scores, just like class grades, have their limitations in terms of the conclusions you can draw.

Administrators are under different pressures than teachers

Another way administrators are different from teachers is administrators are seemingly under yearly pressure to come up with or support some kind of new initiative. As a teacher, you should certainly examine how well a certain teaching strategy worked and if you need to make adjustments to it (or discontinue it altogether), but making change for the sake of change is a bad strategy. Sometimes, things are fine just the way they are. Ships still "set sail," after all. Not so with administrators. Virtually every year, administrators in various schools come up with some new program or philosophical approach to try, along with the corresponding educational jargon that serves to obfuscate rather than clarify. Our suspicion is you'll get the strong impression at times they're just throwing things against the wall to see what sticks. There may be talk about "research-based initiatives," but you shouldn't hold your breath waiting to see such research, even though you may ask for it. You may find new "initiatives" wash up on shore one school year and then float back out with the tide the next and never be heard from again. In fact, there was one nine-year stretch in our career when there were twenty-five different initiatives that came and went. Sometimes changes were actually made, but the entire process seemed quite haphazard. This hit-or-miss approach to different programs also created a distinct disincentive for getting behind those programs completely and energetically. Why bother to put in effort to learn something that isn't going to be around for more than a semester or two?

You'll find these new initiatives get introduced with great fanfare via "professional development," what one teacher described as "a soul-sucking two days of abject boredom" at the beginning of the year. Instead of having time to prepare your classroom for the students, you may find yourself going through what some other teachers have experienced at the start of virtually every year. Approximately 90 percent of the time will be spent on trying to justify why some new nomenclature is now necessary, while the other 10 percent will be spent on activities meant to "engage" the learner (i.e., you). During these professional development days, administrators will typically stand in front of the room, joke about how they "aren't modeling best practices," assure you they won't read word-for-word from a PowerPoint presentation, and then read word-for-word from a PowerPoint presentation. This will probably happen after they stressed the idea of knowing "technology" and then asking the head of the technology department to turn the computer on for their presentation. We're heard a number of different teachers from different districts describe the situation related above. Sadly, we've even attended some of these sessions and have seen the number of teachers looking at their phones instead of at the presenter. Such unprofessional behavior is inexcusable, but too many teachers have told us it happens to view it as an isolated incident.

Administrators evaluate teachers but lack management training

Yet another way administrators differ from teachers is that administrators are supposed to evaluate teachers, despite many lacking the qualifications to do so. A veteran teacher has far more experience in a classroom and understands the nuances of teaching much better than many administrators, yet our experience was that some administrators had a very condescending attitude toward teachers, not respecting the teacher's experience and expertise.

Something is very wrong with a system where a first-year administrator with two year's teaching experience completely disregards the input of a twenty-year teaching veteran. There are obvious exceptions, of course, but you should be aware that the hubris and arrogance of some administrators must truly be experienced to be believed. There also seemed to be the widely held belief that teaching is a one style fits all endeavor. We and other teachers we've talked to were at times given the impression during in-service days that there was some mysterious, inexplicable way of teaching that we were not demonstrating, but no administrator ever explained or demonstrated just what that ethereal teaching method was. It certainly seemed administrators made no allowance for individual differences in teaching styles.

Another area in which administrators differ from teachers and can be sorely lacking is management. In a school setting, "management" simply means an administrator is there to set clear cut goals, communicate what those goals are and why they're beneficial to the students, and help teachers stay focused on and move toward those goals. It's not an easy task, of course, but it's the teachers who ultimately make goals a reality, so any administrator should be a resource for the teachers, helping those teachers buy into and move toward a common good. Keeping all those different personalities pulling in the same direction while handling a number of other duties isn't an enviable task, certainly, but the problem is exacerbated by the fact administrators seem to lack any management training.

The most glaring deficiency administrators had as managers was a lack of clear vision. By that, we mean after a classroom observation, just like during in-service meetings, we (and the vast majority of other teachers we talked to) at times got the distinct impression we weren't teaching the "right" way or meeting that mysterious, unstated standard. When an administrator leaves your room and you get the sense you've done something wrong, it's the responsibility of that administrator to let you know how you didn't meet a specific expectation. Ideally, that administrator would also work with you to help you meet that expectation moving forward. Unfortunately, it seems some administrators are more focused on catching teachers doing something wrong than in helping define specific ways to improve. It doesn't matter how many times an administrator calls you a "team member," if that administrator gives off the vibe that he or she's there to find fault with you, you'll never feel part of the "team" or feel that person's truly there to help you do your job better. Your experience may be different, but regrettably, in our fifty-one combined years of teaching experience, no administrator ever made either one of us a better teacher.

We'd even go so far to say the typical teacher has more true management experience than the average administrator. Besides also dealing with a large number of people every day, teachers are dealing with people who are more volatile and less willing to work toward common goals than adults. In fact, students oftentimes actually work against their own self-interest, and it has to be the teacher who redirects them. Additionally, at least in terms of the faculty, an administrator deals with roughly the same group of people on a yearly basis instead of getting 150 or more new people to work with. Teachers also have to be attuned to individual students' temperaments, a topic we discussed in the first chapter. Highly conscientious students, for example, are extremely self-critical and can't be treated the same way as students lower in conscientiousness. The highly conscientious student doesn't need to be reminded about any low grades or shortcomings. These students need encouragement and need refocused on their strengths and how they can do better in the future. Any teacher worth his or her salt has this ability to handle different people as individuals. Teachers, like administrators, aren't formally trained in managerial techniques, but it's a matter of career survival for teachers to develop those skills quickly, and develop them well.

Administrators aren't your friend (nor should they be)

The final way administrators aren't teachers, and a lesson you would do well to heed from the outset, is that administrators aren't your friend, they're your manager. Your fellow teachers may very well turn out to be your brothers and sisters-in-arms and provide you with invaluable support throughout your career. There are days when other teachers are your sounding board, that shoulder you cry on, or that trusted friend who hears some of the intimate details of your life. Administrators may attempt, in good faith, to be those things for you, but remember you aren't their equal in the organizational hierarchy and their own job may depend on them being an administrator instead of a friend. We've had the distasteful experience of witnessing some administrators pretending to be the teachers' friend one minute and then abruptly transmogrifying into "The Administrator" the next. Thankfully, their efforts were clumsy and obvious, but please be aware your job as a teacher and an administrator's job sometimes clash, and you can be sure they're going to watch out for their own interests above your own.

Remember that some administrators, like some managers, might talk about "coaching up" a "team member" or some similar expression, but they have a way of turning everything back on you. They are correct in the sense that as soon as that classroom door closes, you're on your own. If something bad happens in that room, your immediate supervisor may very well see it as solely your responsibility. Your administrator might then get some heat from the superintendent, but it'll be you who gets 99 percent of the blame. We don't say this to frighten you but to make you aware that rhetoric and reality often don't match in the world of teaching. Unfortunately, it's also the case you might be held responsible for things over which you have no control. For example, one student was referred to an administrator for being chronically absent, so the administrator went to the teacher and asked, "What is it about your class that makes the child not want to come to it?" Another student who was caught cheating on an exam was asked, "What can your teacher do to make you not want to cheat anymore?" In those kinds of situations, there really isn't much you can do except keep exact records of any situation in your classroom and stay on top of any potential trouble.

Concluding thoughts

Despite the differences we've pointed out in this chapter, it's always helpful to keep in mind that administrators are human, too. They have pressure put on them by the superintendent, the parents, the teachers, and the students. They perform different functions than you, so unless you've done their job you should be careful about making snap judgments about them. You should also be sympathetic to the fact that, like teachers, administrators all have their own styles. It's also the case that sometimes they're put in the awkward position of having to follow a district policy with which they don't agree. We found, for example, that some administrators were clearly not comfortable evaluating teachers according to a business model but had to do it anyway (more on teacher evaluation to follow). You can imagine the pressure an administrator would be under if that administrator had to implement a policy he or she felt was deeply flawed. Just like you, sometimes administrators have to grin and bear it when they disagree with the higher-ups. The bottom line is you should try to remember administrators' jobs do differ from yours but that you should all be moving toward the same goal of serving the students.

Chapter 8

GOOD AND BAD ADMINISTRATORS

Introduction

U p to this point, it may seem we've been a little hard on administrators at times, but there are clearly good ones out there, and it's been our pleasure to know some of them. A good administrator looks on teachers as coworkers and has a firm understanding of the challenges facing teachers every day. By challenges, we mean not only students but also parents, administrators, paperwork, and various deadlines that have to be met. A good administrator, like a good manager, has realistic expectations of what a person can do in a given amount of time. We once ran into an irrational administrator who had no understanding of this concept. He wanted to know why two things weren't done at the same time, and when it was explained to him that a minute spent doing one thing is a minute you can't spend doing something else, his response was, "That's not true!" Granted, his is an extreme case, but good administrators realize you can't expect the impossible from others. What you can do, though, is provide teachers with the resources and support necessary to meet school and district goals. Good administrators facilitate the process of teaching whenever possible and don't lose sight of the fact we're all there to educate the students.

Bad administrators, in contrast, normally exhibit poor management skills and put their own interests ahead of anything else, including the students. They're selfish, obviously, and may actually work directly against you in a malicious way. They seem to think their job is so much more difficult and stressful than yours and view you as no more worthy of respect than a child. The worst among are the ones who gleefully see themselves as the "boss" and lord their power over others. The focus of these petty tyrants is so twisted that they aren't interested in doing everything within their power to ensure students have effective teachers. One administrator even made a game of trying to sneak into a teacher's classroom to steal that teacher's roll book (back when such things existed!). Such childishness has no place in a professional setting and is unworthy of anyone charged with supervising others, but such was the focus of this administrator. Sometimes, the behavior of these administrators even works directly against the students they're supposed to be helping. They are the type of people who can't be trusted and are better left alone. There are times when you can't avoid them, though, so you should be aware of some of the forms they may take. In this chapter, we're going to do our best to distinguish between the good and the bad and give you a realistic sense of what your future colleagues may look like.

Good administrators are honest

So, what does a "good" administrator look like? It may sound obvious and simplistic, but one of the qualities of good administrators is that they do what they say they'll do. They explain why they're going to do things a certain way and don't go back on it without good reason. That's not to say they're inflexible, far from it, but it is to say you always know where you stand with an honest administrator. You don't have to agree with everything they do, but you respect the fact they're upfront with you. And the fact they communicate with you shows they respect you as a colleague. Another quality of good administrators is that they can admit when they've made a mistake. Related to acknowledging mistakes is the ability to listen to constructive criticism. Teachers can be smart, too, and have experiences administrators don't. A good administrator listens to teachers' suggestions and, if appropriate, adopts those suggestions even if it means changing a policy the administrator had implemented before. Some people let their ego get in the way and won't take anyone else's suggestion for fear of appearing weak or indecisive, but teachers actually have more respect for administrators who're humble enough and secure enough in themselves to take a good suggestion and run with it.

One such administrator was a principal one of us had. He was a former math teacher who clearly remembered the day-to-day challenges facing us. He had a special gift for focusing on the most significant elements of the job, too. For example, during several meeting he told us the story of how he once took a math test and was very happy because he thought he got all the questions right. When he got the test back, though, the teacher had given him a lower grade because he hadn't aligned all the decimal points for every problem. All of his answers were correct, but the teacher felt his paper didn't look neat enough. He told that story to remind us to focus on what was truly important and not get caught up with minutia. He also wasn't at all hesitant to criticize initiatives from the state if he thought they were vague. Fulfill your obligations, he said, but don't get discouraged by things that truly don't affect the students.

On a more personal note, he also demonstrated to me directly how genuine he was. During his first year as principal, I was diagnosed with cancer and had to undergo surgery. Knowing what kind of person he was, I felt comfortable calling him the day of the surgery to tell him everything had gone well. He was absolutely thrilled, and every time I saw him after that he asked me about my health before discussing anything else and even gave me a playful "punch" on the arm as he congratulated me on my recovery.

He was eventually promoted to a higher position in the district but still sought me out at district meetings to ask if I was doing well. It's hard to forget someone like him going out of his way to show such consideration and kindness. We didn't always agree on policy, but I trusted his judgment and admired his humanity. He respected my opinions and seriously wanted my input, and that's something that has always stood out. Tellingly, during my entire teaching career, not one other administrator ever asked for my opinion or feedback on anything.

Good administrators support you

A lot has been made about teacher salaries and working conditions, but for as long as we can remember teachers who've left the job have said the lack of support was the most significant factor in their decision. When teachers talk about "lack of support," they mean various things, but the most important are feeling understood and appreciated. If both administrators and parents are sympathetic to the fact that the job is highly stressful and teachers need encouragement and a sense that someone has their back, then the teachers will feel supported. There are a lot of jobs out there that are less stressful than teaching and pay a comparable amount, so feeling other people understand what you're going through and are pulling for you is important. Teachers need to feel they truly are part of a team that's working together to educate the students.

One such administrator comes to mind immediately. It may sound strange, but our most vivid memory of her had to do with a male security guard. This gentleman was the epitome of professionalism and normally was on a very even keel. One day, though, he came into the administrator's office, obviously fuming. Our administrator simply said, "Mr. So-and-so, you look like somebody really pissed you off." He admitted that someone had and vented for a couple of minutes, with the administrator just listening. They joked about it afterward, and the security guard left the office much calmer. Both security guards and teachers have those days when kids get under their skin, and sometimes, they just need a sympathetic ear. A good administrator lets you vent when you need to vent and doesn't turn it back on you. There have been cases when a teacher has complained to an administrator about a classroom situation only to have the administrator show up the next day to conduct a formal observation of that class, not to assess the situation and offer guidance, but to find out what the teacher was doing "wrong." Good administrators are there to listen to other adults who're having a rough day, not to somehow look for a weakness and punish them for it. That's what support looks like.

Another thing that made this particular administrator special was the fact she was approachable and genuine. She had her bad days, too, and she wasn't shy about showing she was human, too. She also knew quite well that some kids really misbehave and that some parents are completely unreasonable. If you had a problem with a student or parent, she listened and considered your viewpoint instead of treating you with smug condescension. Her assumption was that we all needed to support each other for the benefit of everyone: administrators, teachers, students, and community. A huge part of that approach was building relationships. You never got the feeling you were an inferior but rather a colleague whose opinion was valued. She never forgot how hard a teacher's job is and how we had to be on the same page to make the school work. Again, that's what support looks like.

Good administrators respect you

When I was a twenty-seven-year-old first year teacher, I ran into a situation where a student's behavior warranted sending the student to the assistant principal. The student was clearly in the wrong, calling me a "motherf-cker" and having to be led out of class by a security office. After class, I met with the assistant principal and the student. The first thing the administrator did was turn to me and say, "Let's hear your side of the story." I was immediately taken aback by the phrasing of the question. By wording the question the way she did, the administrator was putting me on equal footing with the child, which struck me as very wrong. In the administrator's eyes, my "version" of what happened in class carried no more weight than the student's version. That was the very first time I had ever dealt directly with an administrator, and it was then I realized not all administrators would treat me like an adult and with the respect I deserved.

We think other teachers would agree that one of the most important things an administrator can do when dealing with teachers, if not the most important thing, is respect them. By respecting teachers, we mean administrators should assume teachers have experience and knowledge that the administrator doesn't. An administrator may have taught for two years before moving on to be an assistant principal, but that doesn't mean that person knows more than someone who's been in a classroom for fifteen years. We'd bet money they don't. By way of illustration, a person who has taught in an inner-city school for fifteen years very likely has a great deal of skill, good judgment, and discretion when dealing with students, parents, and other adults. We base that assumption on the fact that such qualities are vital to surviving in an environment in which there is day-to-day verbal abuse from students and pushback against any and all learning activities. Until the teacher proves otherwise, we would afford that teacher due respect.

It also doesn't require a ton of effort to demonstrate that respect. One year, after a lot of emphasis was put on providing formative assessments, I approached an administrator and asked him if he could provide me with some examples of formative assessments I could use in my classroom. For those who don't know, a formative assessment is any activity that lets you know if and how well your students understand what you're teaching them before you give them a final test or project. (this definition was pieced together after fourteen fumbling hours of in-service meetings, which should give you a sense of how valuable some of those meetings are.) We hadn't had any dealings with each other before, but he seemed like a nice, friendly person. Within a week, he gave me a packet of about two dozen detailed examples of formative assessments for use in the classroom. He had even taken the time to highlight ones he thought would be the most helpful to me. I really appreciated him going to the trouble of putting a packet together and giving me his input without coming across as telling me what to do. The entire process seemed very much like a collaboration, which is exactly how the relationship with an administrator should work. I also appreciated him highlighting the ones he liked because I was sure to use them during my next observation. I did that so no other administrator could criticize them and say I was doing the wrong thing. Maybe that was a tad cynical on my part, but sometimes, it helps to be a savvy veteran!

Another administrator who took a collaborative approach helped me out with an interpersonal conflict with another teacher. The other teacher was only willing to discuss things because an administrator had asked him to, but the process went well. During the meeting, this particular administrator simply asked some guiding questions and listened carefully to both of us. He wasn't sitting there acting like some kind of judge or arbiter, but rather as a third-party with a sympathetic ear for both of us. In the end, the other teacher was unwilling to work out the conflict, but I certainly appreciated the fact this administrator respected both of us enough to hear us out and offer some suggestions. I also appreciated the fact this administrator kept our entire conversation in confidence. Once again, respect was shown for both of us, even though the situation between us wasn't resolved.

Good administrators remember why they're there

Make no mistake, just like teachers, administrators are going 100 mph from the minute they walk into school every day. They have to sneak out for bathroom breaks, skip lunch, stay late, and take work home. They also work during the summer. Given these demands, no one should blame administrators if they get overwhelmed at times. Despite immense demands on their time, the good administrators remember they're there for the ultimate benefit of the students. They see the "big picture" of the students' lives and don't get lost in all the minutia of the day. Everyone has demands on them and can be excused for temporarily losing focus on the big picture, but a good administrator is able to bring the focus back to the fact we're working with kids and have a tremendous obligation to look out for them and aid them along their life's journey.

A great example of such an administrator involves one who might very well have changed the course of a young woman's life by taking ten minutes out of his day. This particular administrator was walking by the attendance office one day and happened to see a senior who'd cut school one too many times. He pulled her out of the attendance line and explained how he'd been "just like you" and how she was going to fail high school unless she went to her gym teacher and convinced him to let her work really hard the second semester in order to pass. He also was very upfront with her, telling her if she missed one more day of school she was going to fail on attendance. We consider him a good administrator because even though he was the principal of the school and had dozens of things pulling him different ways, he took the time to single out someone who had a lot of potential but was in danger of blowing it. With all the other students he had to deal with, it would've been very easy and understandable if she had simply "slipped through the cracks." This administrator made sure that didn't happen. The story also has a happy ending because the young lady in question eventually wound up becoming a very successful local business owner. She credits his intervention as a crossroads in her life where he helped her take the right path and not wind up like a friend of hers who didn't make the right choice. A good administrator notices and makes time for that struggling student whom other administrators would ignore.

Bad administrators are dishonest

What, then, do "bad" administrators look like? Regrettably, dishonesty is a common quality among too many people, but the dishonest administrator can make your life a living hell. One principal began the school year by stressing how everyone was on the same team and how the administration was there to support teachers. She further said she wanted special emphasis placed on curbing cell phone use and encouraged teachers to write behavioral referrals for any student who was a chronic abuser of cell phones in class. She emphasized that they wouldn't be counting the number of referrals teachers sent and that teachers should go ahead and send as many as needed. In mid-October, however, teachers who'd written referrals for cell phone use were called into her office and asked why they had written so many referrals. The principal took the position that any teacher who wrote so many referrals must not have control of the class. As you can imagine, referrals for cell phone use dried up immediately, and phones became a major issue in the school. Our point here isn't to condemn cell phone use in schools, which can certainly have its place, but to highlight how administrators can directly contradict their own policies and blame you for following those policies.

Another example of administrator dishonesty has to do with an upper-level class. The teacher involved had been teaching a number of years but several administrators gave vague hints that the class was too difficult. When the teacher asked them directly if they wanted him to make it easier, they immediately protested that they didn't. During that same time, many of the older teachers were retiring and were being replaced with younger teachers who didn't hold the students to the same academic standards. The older teacher was assured several times, though, that they wanted him to keep the upper-level class "rigorous." The entire time these conversations were going on, these same administrators still hinted that students should be given better grades and not have to work as hard. This game went on for several years until the older teacher was assigned a different class. The teacher who replaced him immediately lowered the academic standards significantly, and that was the last of it. Our assumption is that parents were complaining that the class was too hard, but the administrators weren't honest enough to ask the teacher to dumb the class down. We certainly hope we're mistaken, but we've heard various teachers from various districts relate similar stories.

Bad administrators live in dread of disgruntled parents

Especially toward the end of our careers, we noticed an increasing number of administrators who lived in abject fear of displeasing any parent. If an angry parent came into the school, teachers used to joke about how administrators hid under their desks. For as brave and fierce as these administrators were when confronting teachers, they were absolute cowards when it came to the parents. We need to be careful here, though, because school officials are walking a tightrope when dealing with parents. Parents have a serious stake in what goes on in the school, and it's their taxes that're paying the freight for all school employees. They have a right to be heard and respected, without question. There are some parents, however, who're unreasonable and simply can't be catered to. As a teacher, there're times when you're going to have to set clear limits on some parents, and administrators should be willing to do the same. Unfortunately, our experience has been that even the most unreasonable parent can sometimes be accommodated far beyond what is appropriate or helpful. A quick example should illustrate this point.

After school one day, two administrators came into a teacher's classroom without saying anything or making eye contact. The teacher found that quite odd since it's customary to greet people when you walk into a room. I remember from a college Psychology class the professor mentioned that approaching people in silence is perceived as a threat, so the teacher involved must've known something was up. Puzzled, the teacher watched them turned two of the desks toward him, sit down with their computers, and start typing. It felt as if it were some sort of court of inquiry. As one of them dutifully typed down the proceedings, the other asked the teacher if he'd like to comment on "the incident" that happened in the classroom earlier that day. The teacher responded in all honesty that he had no idea what incident the administrator meant. Huffily, the administrator explained that earlier in the day the teacher had moved a student's backpack and the administration wanted to know why such a thing had been done. Apparently, the backpack in question was blocking one of the aisles and the teacher had nearly tripped over it. The teacher then pushed the backpack under the student's desk. Apparently, the student whose backpack had been moved was very upset about it and had complained to one of the parents. Livid, the parent called the principal, and the principal sent these administrators running to investigate.

Eventually, the teacher had to meet with the principal and one of the other administrators who'd met with him previously. The principal simply kept repeating in feigned disbelief, "I don't know why anyone would ever touch a child's backpack" but added nothing to the situation. It was finally decided that another phone call with the parent was necessary. With a look of sheer terror on his face, one of the administrators said, "*I'm* not going to call her." The teacher courageously put himself forward to make the two-minute phone call, resolved the situation, and apparently put all the planets and stars back into proper order. The pompous self-importance and mock gravitas of those administrators would have been laughable if it weren't so pathetic. You may never run into such a tempest in a teacup, but just be aware that some administrators live in absolute fear of parents. If there's ever any kind of issue with a parent, you can be sure they won't support you.

Bad administrators want to make their lives easier

Most people probably want their lives to be easier, and teachers are certainly no exception. There's a difference, though, between wanting to ease your stress level a bit and making your own comfort the main focus of your job. Unfortunately, we've run into several administrators who fit that description. Two people, in particular, come to mind. One tried to make his life easier by ignoring student misbehavior as much as possible so he wouldn't have to fill out paperwork, call parents, and, of course, have unpleasant encounters with students. This administrator came into my classroom one day during my preparation period, all in a huff, and complained about how I'd written too many behavioral referrals. Anticipating just such an occurrence, I calmly opened one of my desk drawers, pulled out copies I had made of the referrals, and started to go through each of them one by one, asking him if each referral had been appropriate. By way of reference, I think the first referral had to do with one student throwing a chair at another student and threatening to kill her, and the others weren't much better. After going through two or three of these referrals, he threw his hands, said, "We're not doing this," and walked out of the room. This administrator had a penchant for putting chronically misbehaving students back in class without any consequences, allowing them to continue to disrupt the education of other students.

Incidentally, you should also take note once again of how this administrator wanted to talk about statistics instead of individual students. On the surface, it looked very bad for me that I had written so many referrals, but if you looked at each individual case, it was clear that the referrals were necessary. In terms of the incident when one student threw a chair at another student, if either student had gotten hurt and I hadn't written a referral, it would have been my job on the line. We would recommend you take our approach and never draw conclusions about an individual student based on group statistics. Don't be afraid to remind administrators that each student is unique and deserves to be treated as an individual and not some sort of statistic. Any administrator who does such a thing is, quite frankly, short-changing kids in order to make his or her own life easier.

Another administrator who was trying to make his life easier was a principal who had a unique way of dealing with accusations against teachers. He called one of us into his office one day to explain how a student had accused us of saying some inappropriate things in front of the class. He had already called in each student in the class, talked to them individually, and found that the accusation was completely false. He made me aware of the situation, said that the accusation had no basis in fact, but that he was going to keep the accusation in my file just in case it "showed a pattern." When I protested it wasn't fair or accurate to keep false accusations on file, he simply said I could write a letter of rebuttal and put it in my personnel file. We're going to be generous here and chalk his behavior up to wanting to take the path of least resistance and cover himself, rather than outright maliciousness. Still, this administrator showed no regard for how damaging a false accusation can be against a teacher and simply documented it to make his life easier.

There are some administrators who are so interested in the path of least resistance for themselves that have no regard for the education of students. The most morally repugnant of these administrators actually used blackmail in an effort to get a student's grade changed. The student in question was a Special Education student who wasn't happy with the grade he earned in a class. He pleaded on a couple of occasions to have his grade raised, but the numbers didn't justify it. Over the summer, however, the teacher received a phone call from an administrator. The administrator said the parents wanted the grade changed because, "It wouldn't look good on a college transcript." Dumbfounded, the teacher explained how the grade was valid and how all assignments had already been turned in. The administrator insisted the grade be changed to what the parents wanted, but the conversation quickly led to an impasse.

It was at that point the administrator threatened that unless the grade was changed, a disciplinary hearing would be held because, "The student's IEP was violated." She also said that if the grade *was* changed, no such hearing would be held and the matter would be resolved. Without going into the drawn out and sordid details, the situation ended with the parents getting the exact grade they wanted for their child. We wonder how many other grades had been changed for this student either before or after that class. We also wonder whether this student got into a college for which he wasn't even remotely qualified. The fact that such things can be legitimately contemplated speaks poorly for that administrator and the atmosphere she was responsible for creating.

Bad administrators can harass you or your fellow teachers

The most revolting example of blatant disrespect we can think of had to do with what we consider a case of sexual harassment. There was one administrator who had zero respect for women. He used to walk into the teachers' lounge, look at a woman, tap his fingers on the coffee maker, and simply say, "Coffee." Besides demanding coffee, he also had a habit of openly leering at younger teachers and made comments of an explicit sexual nature when those female teachers weren't around. After one too many times of him tapping and asking for coffee, a teacher spoke up and said, "Mr. So-and-so, it isn't anybody's job to make you coffee. We are all equals here." He didn't say anything in response, and after he left the room, a female teacher looked at the teacher, smiled, and said, "Oh, that's just the way he is."

If you ever find yourself in such a situation, you'll probably give serious thought to filing sexual harassment charges against anyone like that, which we believe is appropriate. Sadly, though, sexual harassment charges are a tricky thing, and filing such charges can certainly backfire on you. You can be seen as a troublemaker and "not a team player." If you ever find yourself in such a situation, you really are going to have to decide for yourself whether it's worth filing such charges. A lot will depend on the circumstances surrounding the person, your school environment, and whether or not you're ready to deal with the backlash. We wish we could advise you in a more direct way, but it's simply an area with too many possible outcomes to predict. The only rule of thumb we would give you is don't ever tolerate someone touching you in a sexual way, propositioning you, or threatening your job unless you provide them with sexual favors. Hopefully, you'll never find yourself in such a situation, but you should be aware there are still people out there in positions of power who will abuse those powers if given the chance.

Concluding thoughts

Despite some of the horror stories we've related, our hope is you'll develop cooperative and productive relationships with the administrators you run across. Each teacher's experience is unique, so yours may be better or worse than ours, but for the sake of your career's longevity and for the sake of the kids you'll teach let's again hope your experience will be one of the better ones. If you do run into an administrator who lies, disrespects you, or is simply there to collect a paycheck, realize you'll most likely have to grin and bear it. Remind yourself that interactions with administrators are only a fraction of your time compared to your interactions with your students and that the vast majority of your focus should be on your kids. If you are unfortunate enough to find an administrator who interferes with or is destructive of that time with your students, then at that point you'll have to make the decision of whether to batten down the hatches and wait for fairer weather, transfer to another school, or leave the teaching field altogether. It's a shame that one bad administrator could actually influence you to make such a drastic move as a career change, but we've both seen it happen numerous times. We wish you the best of luck in your own career, though!

Chapter 9

HOW TEACHERS ARE EVALUATED

Introduction

Think about a great teacher you've known. What made that teacher such a great teacher? Was it anything you could put a number on or easily compare among 100 other teachers, or was it something rather unique to the person that couldn't exactly be duplicated by somebody else? It's not like a doctor replacing a person's hip; how a student does or does not "click" with a teacher happens on such an individual level that it's difficult if not impossible to quantify. Maybe you were that student who never had an interest in a math class but then all of a sudden exceled in Geometry while the student sitting right next to you didn't. Was it the teacher? Was it the subject matter? Was it because you were older and had matured as a student? Was it some other factor or factors? And if we do credit the teacher for your sudden interest and aptitude in Geometry, how confident should we be in assigning that credit in some measurable fashion? As we pointed out in the previous chapter, there're a number of considerations involved before we can separate the "good" teachers from the "bad," and our experience has been that these issues are far more complex than current evaluations for teachers allow. In this chapter, we're going to keep with the theme of difficulties in measuring teacher effectiveness, but we're also going to get more specific and give you an idea of how you might be evaluated. We certainly recommend you familiarize yourself with how a district evaluates its teachers before accepting a position in that district.

Regardless of which district you decide to work for, certain behaviors of "good" teachers are rather straightforward to evaluate (e.g., assessing whether students are grasping the material). Perhaps your prospective district has given serious thought to which specific behaviors it expects its teachers to exhibit, but we have yet to hear any district or state articulate its thought process. We certainly believe the public should be fully aware of the process and have a district or state explain its rationale for using the criteria it uses. Some elements of good teaching simply can't even be measured or quantified, but you do need to identify and measure what you can. Hopefully, your prospective district doesn't have an evaluation system that's overly ambitious, but one that serves the needs of students in a real way. Calling something research-based, data-driven, or research-driven doesn't automatically give it any credibility at all. Evaluation models of teachers desperately want to give off an air of scientific precision, but our argument is that you can only get so precise when you're dealing with the learning process or with teacher evaluation, and that's okay. We should certainly do everything we can to research teacher evaluation models, but we must always recognize the limitations of such research. As one person eloquently put it, "If you can't convince them with the facts, bedazzle them with bullshit." Our hope is that your district sticks to the facts.

How you'll be evaluated, generally

Regardless of which specific evaluation system your district will use, either created by the administrators of that district or education specialists of the state, it will take the format of a rubric. A rubric is simply a scoring guide of behaviors or expectations you're to meet, along with a brief explanation of what those behaviors or expectations entail. In a simplistic rubric, if you meet all the requirements of that rubric, you'll either be given a score of "satisfactory" or "unsatisfactory." Rubrics normally are more complex than that, though, and normally distinguish among those who go beyond the expectations, those who meet it, those who need improvement, and those who are failing to meet a minimum standard. If you think about it in an educational setting, a rubric, in theory at least, should distinguish an "A" from a "B" from a "C" and so on. Teachers use rubrics all the time to let the students know ahead of time how to earn the highest grades. For teacher evaluation, rubrics are supposed to serve the same purpose and distinguish the excellent teachers from the good teachers, the good from the average, the average from the poor, and the poor from the failing.

A clearly worded rubric that allows you to assess a superior performance all the way down to a failing performance is very valuable for teachers, students, and parents. If you assign an essay in English class, for example, a rubric should benefit students because they'll know ahead of time exactly what you want in the essay, it'll help you because those essays will be of a presumably higher quality, and it'll aid parents in both helping their child craft a superior essay and understanding the final grade assigned to the essay. Given such potential benefits of rubrics, then, it makes perfect sense for a state or district to want to apply one to evaluating teachers. After all, the purpose of a rubric is to aid someone in achieving an excellent performance, not as a way to assign fault or blame after the fact. Absolutely critical to the success of a rubric, then, is that it be written with its expectations outlined clearly, that those who will be evaluated by it (and to those who will do the evaluating) are familiar and comfortable with it, and that it be discussed during any meeting after it's been applied. We believe the entire purpose of evaluating teachers is to ensure students have the best education possible, so creation of a proper rubric for teacher evaluation is critical.

Unfortunately, our experience with teacher evaluation rubrics has been negative. The rubrics applied during our careers were so cumbersomely worded and incredibly general that they weren't helpful. We were never exactly sure how to achieve the highest scores or even, at times, what distinguished an exemplary teacher from an unsatisfactory one. It would be instructive for you to do a little research on the specific language of teacher evaluation rubrics in your state to see if our experiences apply in your individual case. Our guess is, unfortunately, you'll quickly find there's quite a bit of vague language that can be interpreted in a variety of ways. Besides being vague and open to multiple interpretations, it's also appropriate to note that you, as a teacher, could never use such vague scoring guidelines for your students. If you believe a student earned a "B" instead of an "A" and the parent asks you why their child didn't get the "A," you darn well better be able to explain why or you're in trouble.

Vaguely worded rubrics also leave too much room for administrator bias. For example, if your evaluation model rates you on thirty-five different components, an administrator may ask you to provide evidence for each of those thirty-five components within one lesson, which is impossible. Right away, we run into issues of reliability. If several administrators evaluate you at the same time and each chooses to focus on different components, their evaluations may be wildly different. There's also a danger an administrator may choose to ask for a component he or she knows wasn't in the lesson simply because that administrator doesn't like the teacher. Ideally, the administrator would give you an idea ahead of time which components of the rubric you should focus on, but that isn't always the case. You should be aware that in teaching, as in other occupations, you may be evaluated unfairly. One simple way to guard against such a thing is allowing teachers to choose who will do their evaluation, so maybe your prospective district allows for that. If the rubric is truly objective and the principal trusts all the administrators to be fair, then there shouldn't be an issue with allowing teachers to do just that. If 90 percent of your teachers choose one administrator, then there's a good chance you know either something is not equitable with your administrative staff or the rubric you're using is flawed. Unfortunately, our experience was administrators were more focused on "catching" teachers doing something imperfectly than helping them become better teachers. That approach is completely wrong, as any successful business person would tell you. Although not always true, it's generally easier and more desirable to help an employee improve job performance than it is to recruit, train, and retain a new employee.

Informal and formal observations

In terms of how rubrics are applied, they'll be used to rate you as "Satisfactory" or "Unsatisfactory" based on classroom observations or on classroom observations and required documentation, such as a lesson portfolio. If you are using a satisfactory or unsatisfactory scale for your state, each semester's rating is essentially a pass/fail system. Your score on the rubric will be based on classroom observations. These observations take one of two forms, the casual or "walk-through" observation and the formal observation. "Walk-through" observations are typically no big deal and shouldn't worry a competent teacher. An administrator or administrators will pop into your classroom, stay for five to ten minutes, and then leave. Within a day or two you'll get an email or a note in your mailbox giving you a few sentences of feedback on your lesson. You can expect to get two to three such observations per year. You should be on your guard with walk-through observations, though, because administrators sometimes use such observations as a pretext for a formal observation. It's also the case that the threat of a formal observation is used as a way to intimidate teachers. Such abuse of an evaluation system is unfair and counterproductive to staff morale, but we've both seen it happen, unfortunately. You don't want to become paranoid about observations, but do take them seriously. If you're doing what you should be doing every day, such observations shouldn't worry you.

You should also get two formal observations, one each semester. As a new teacher, your administrator may decide you need three formal observations, but they should all follow the same format. Hopefully, a formal observation will include a pre-observation conference and a post-observation conference. During the pre-observation conference, the administrator will tell you what he or she will be looking for during the lesson and also may ask you how the lesson fits in with the school's curriculum. It's at this conference you should ask any questions about the rubric used or about what's expected of you. You should leave that meeting feeling comfortable about what's to come. During the post-observation conference, you'll be asked to discuss how you thought the lesson went, what could've gone better, and what changes, if any, you'd make to the lesson in the future. The administrator will then give you feedback on the strengths and weaknesses of the lesson. Ideally, the post-observation conference is useful for future lessons and professional growth. You shouldn't dread these observations or conferences but simply see them as part of your job. Unless you did something dreadfully wrong, you'll be fine. And even if you did screw up royally and have to have another formal observation, that's appropriate. The students deserve to have high quality teaching, so admit it to yourself if the lesson was a disaster and do better next time!

Is it possible for one terrible formal observation to turn out as a catastrophe for your career? The short answer is "yes," but there's a process involved. If you do have the misfortune of a lesson going completely sideways during a formal observation, you'll be given more chances. Typically, you'll be put on some kind of improvement plan and assigned someone to guide you in improving your performance. Once you've demonstrated to the satisfaction of the administration you've met the standards of the improvement plan, you'll be taken off of that plan and things go back to "normal." If your performance fails to improve, you'll be given an "unsatisfactory" rating for the semester. Things aren't over at that point, though. You'll be given another semester to demonstrate your competence as a teacher, which will include more chances to meet with a mentor or administrator of some sort who, in theory anyway, is a resource for you. If you fail to meet the standards of the improvement plan for two semesters in a row, your employment will, typically, be terminated.

Before you panic about formal observations, though, it's helpful to give a little thought to the matter. Formal observations shouldn't be any great obstacle for a veteran teacher. If you've been at your job for several years or more, you've no doubt demonstrated your competence on a number of occasions. If you were truly unsatisfactory as a teacher, a student, parent, or administrator would've made an issue of it earlier in your career. Everyone can have a bad day, obviously, but for a veteran teacher to go through two full semesters and not demonstrate basic ability as a teacher would be strange, indeed. What happens, though, if you have a new administrator who has it in for you for whatever reason? It's at that point you should get your union involved, assuming you belong to one. A union can't prevent a bad teacher from being terminated, but a union can ensure a teacher is being treated according to the collective bargaining agreement between the district and the teachers. Our experience was that such intervention by a union representative was very rare, but you should have an idea of how to protect yourself from unfair treatment. You might also want to consider protecting yourself ahead of time by creating a professional portfolio, containing evidence of things like lesson plans, differentiated assignments, any effective assessment tools you have used, and any positive communications with parents. If the parents take the time to send you a short note thanking you for working with their child, for example, save the email to your portfolio file. Besides being there if you to submit evidence of parent communication to an administrator, keeping those kinds of emails can also be a great pick-me-up if you are having a bad day or a bad week.

What happens, though, if you're in your first year of teaching and find yourself with an unsatisfactory rating? Such things happen, of course, though they really shouldn't. Unfortunately, there are some rather perverse incentives at work that allow inadequate teachers to slip through the cracks and wind up in a classroom. Colleges and universities, for example, don't have a system in place to weed out the bad teachers until those teachers reach their practicum, either a one-semester student teaching stint or a full-year internship. During those experiences, the college or university will have a representative of their Education Department involved to provide some guidance. Think of the situation that representative is in, though. After allowing a student to go through three years of an Education program, would a representative of that program truly want to tell a student he or she just didn't have what it takes to be a teacher? Besides wanting to protect the Education Department, such a representative, unless they're inhuman, would probably feel uncomfortable on some level crushing another person's career dreams.

A similar situation exists for the cooperating or supervising teacher at the school. Both of us have had student teachers and have witnessed our colleagues with student teachers. You're not doing student teachers a favor by giving them a positive recommendation if they aren't qualified teachers, but we've witnessed several of our colleagues provide such recommendations. Part of why they gave an undeserved recommendation was they didn't to kill someone's career prospects after that person had invested so much time and money into the endeavor. Another aspect of giving an undeserved recommendation was these cooperating or supervising teachers didn't want to be seen as poor mentors. Teachers have enough on their plate without having to deal with an enraged student teacher and the college or university supervisor, so it's easier to simply pass along the problem to someone else. We certainly condemn such behavior, but we'd be lying if we said we never saw it happen. If you do find yourself in such a situation, passed along despite not being up for the job, try not to take it personally. Not everyone is suited to be a teacher, and it's better to find out sooner rather than later that the job simply isn't for you. Despite the time you've already invested in getting that Education degree or that teaching certificate, it's nothing compared to being in a job you hate for the next thirty-five years.

Let's assume, though, like most teachers, you're perfectly competent and find yourself experiencing a formal observation. What's it like? The first thing you should understand is that formal observations, like the name implies, are structured a certain way and will have certain components (the pre-observation conference being one). Unlike a walk-through observation, the administrator will stay for the entire class period. The students know you'll be putting on a dog-and-pony show for the administrator, and the sympathetically minded students will help you out by raising their hands more than normal and volunteering for any activities. You'll give silent thanks for those kinds of students, but remember to try to engage as many students as possible, not just the ones who're actively trying to help you. In terms of the administrator, you'll also notice that person spending all of the time typing. What that person is doing is recording, as much as possible, everything you do and say during the lesson. And by "everything," we mean they're trying to create a word-for-word transcript of what you say, where you walk in the classroom, who you call on, and even your hand gestures. We'll stress again that you be mindful of which students you call on. If you're teaching math or science and only call on male students, you'll definitely hear about it during your post-observation conference. The same is true if you don't call on minority students. You shouldn't ignore students of any kind during your typical lesson, of course, but realize the administrator will actually be counting the number of students you call on and which group they fall into, so do so with care.

Quite frankly, neither of use was ever comfortable with this style of observation for several reasons. First, unless the administrators are trained stenographers, you can't be sure what they're writing down is accurate. It would be very easy for speech to be taken out of context. Second, the whole idea of writing down (supposedly) everything you say strikes us as too close to "everything you say can and will be used against you." Knowing that even the smallest verbal slip up will be recorded and used against you later is unnerving and makes you rather self-conscious. You're thinking so much about how what you're saying might be interpreted that it throws off your concentration on the students, which is counterproductive to the whole process. Finally, focusing so much on the minutiae of the lesson is the exact opposite of good note-taking. A competent teacher would never recommend students scramble and try to type down every single word of a lesson. We understand administrators are desperate for "evidence" during their observations, but they're no doubt missing the overall flow and impact of the lesson. It's akin to writing down the individual notes but not listening to the music.

After the formal observation, you'll be called in for a conference with the administrator. It's at this meeting the administrator will ask you how you thought the lesson went, what you would change for next time, and if you have any questions. The administrator *should* tell you not only what you did well during the lesson but also how the lesson could be improved. Don't get thrown off by criticism, though. Administrators *have* to find something "wrong" with your lesson, no matter how small. That's when the transcript of what you said or did might be referenced. You might also be asked hypothetical situations, such as how you would "differentiate" instruction for all learners or allow for "equity" in your classroom. Those terms can mean different things to different people, so make sure you're clear on what the administrator's looking for before you answer. The administrator may take offence at you asking for a clarification of a term, but it's better to be seen as obtuse rather than giving the "wrong" answer that will get you in trouble. If we're coming off as sounding a little paranoid at this point, realize we've seen too many instances of teachers being put under a microscope because they didn't repeat administrative talking points. Administrators are not your friends, they're your supervisors, and their incentives are different from yours. Protect yourself.

Examples of evaluation models

In terms of specific models for teacher evaluation, a very well-know and popular one was advanced by Charlotte Danielson, and you may find your district bases at least some of your evaluation on her ideas. The Danielson model evaluates teachers based on four "domains." These domains are Planning and Preparation, Classroom Environment, Instruction, and Professional Responsibility. Under each of these domains, there are a number of components, sometimes thirty or more, each of which can be used for evaluation. If your district utilizes a system based on the Danielson model, each of those components should be spelled out for you. Please make sure you ask any questions you have, though, since an observer may be looking for anywhere from 1 to 120 or more specific things during your observation. We've cautioned before about how vaguely worded rubrics are an issue, and the same is true of Danielson-based models. We don't mean that as a personal criticism of Danielson but as a realization that there are districts out there that haven't personalized teacher evaluation models for their own situation and students. There's real room for abuse with any vague evaluation model or model that has over 100 individual parts, so it's important you ask about any aspect of your evaluation you aren't sure about. We believe it's very important for teachers to have faith in both the validity and the fairness of any evaluation model, so make sure you're clear on what's expected of you for any of the following domains.

The first domain of the Danielson model is Planning and Preparation, which concentrates on what a teacher does before entering the classroom. As you gather from the name, an important part of evaluating teachers is making sure they've put careful thought into why a lesson is necessary, how it fits in with the unit being taught, and whether or not it conforms to the educational standards of the district and/or state. The teacher should also demonstrate competence in collecting and organizing any materials necessary for the lesson. Quite frankly, any competent teacher should get high marks in this domain. You should have a clear understanding of what you're teaching and why, and you most certainly should be able to justify each and every one of your lessons to students, parents, and administrators. As a first or second-year teacher, though, meeting the Planning and Preparation standard will be a lot more difficult. There're only so many hours in the day, so unless your school has a specific curriculum outlined for you ahead of time, you'll have to plan out your entire course, which can be an overwhelming process.

Courses should be planned out in a top-down fashion, which is incredibly time consuming. By top-down, we mean you should figure out how many units of study you'll cover during the year and how many class periods you'll spend on each unit. If you're teaching U.S. History, for example, you need to decide in August what you'll be teaching by the beginning of June. You'll need to count up the number of days you have to work with (e.g., 180 days), where in history you want to wind up, and how many days you're going to devote to each unit of study. If you want to finish the year with a unit on the early 2000s, for example, you have to make sure you're not still teaching the Civil War in March. Once you've identified the individual units and how many days you're going to devote to each, you need to plan out the specific lesson sequence for each unit. The final step in that process is planning an individual lesson. Given the pressures and demands, though, beginning teachers normally follow this process backwards and scramble around trying to figure out what they'll do the next day or the upcoming week. Most teachers have probably found themselves in this predicament, though, so do your best and realize you'll continually be tweaking your lessons. You should certainly sit down at the end of each year and reflect on how you can improve your planning and preparation for the next year.

The second of Danielson's domains is the Classroom Environment, which refers to the physical arrangement and milieu of your classroom. In simple terms, this domain is concerned with not only how you organize your room to best facilitate learning, but also with how you treat your students and how they treat each other. Mutual respect is a key element for this domain, and that respect applies to student-to-student interactions. A proper classroom environment means the students are attentive to the teacher and to each other, ask pertinent questions, and actively engage in class activities. Any sort of off-task behavior is dealt with discreetly and with sensitivity, and there's a feeling of cooperation and "buy in" for the students. Ideally, the classroom environment makes all students feel welcome, accepted, and valued both by the teacher and by their fellow students. As noted before, it's also a good idea to greet students by name as they come in the door. We suggest doing that every day, anyway, because it helps establish an environment of acceptance and welcome, but it's also something an observer would most likely look for.

This particular domain can be much harder to negotiate than Planning and Preparation, as you might already have guessed, because so much of it is out of your control. Even how you arrange your room, physically, may be limited by the size or shape of your room. Our experience was there was an unspoken rule that your score in this domain would be lower if your desks were arranged in standard rows. Administrators wanted to see desks in a circle or horseshoe arrangement in order to "facilitate discussion," and any other arrangement got you lower marks. If you're in a biology, chemistry, or physics lab, though, it may be impossible for you to rearrange desks/tables. It's also the case not every lesson requires discussion, but if you're being formally observed we'd suggest you have students talking to each other and responding to what other students say in order to get better marks for your evaluation. This element of the domain is clearly out of your control. If it's Monday morning, first period, it's not the teacher's fault students are half asleep and not too willing to talk. You can bet your evaluation marks will be lower, though, if the students aren't as "engaged" as the rubric wants, so just hope your observation comes later in the week and later in the day. We question the validity and fairness of evaluating teachers based on what the students do, but such is the system you'll most likely have.

The third of Danielson's domains is Instruction, which is concerned with how you communicate the content to your students, how you engage them in the lesson, and how you demonstrate flexibility in adapting the lesson to your individual students. In other words, are you "checking for understanding" as you're going along, paying attention to what the students are saying to you and to each other, and are you changing any part of the lesson that just doesn't seem to be working. This domain can also be rather tricky to score well in because you can't anticipate everything that'll happen during the class. Students aren't just going to sit there like heads of cabbage (hopefully not, anyway!), so they'll understand some things faster than you anticipated or struggle with concepts you thought were rather basic, they'll ask questions, they'll be distracted during the lesson or try to distract others, and behave in ways you simply can't plan for. As you know from your own experiences as a student, some teachers handle such classroom dynamics seamlessly and seemingly effortlessly while others get flustered and thrown off track. You really should be adept in this domain, though, because part of good teaching if having the flexibility to deviate from a preplanned lesson, if necessary. The whole point is to teach students, not to get through a body of information in an arbitrary time period. Asking, "Does anybody have any questions?" isn't good enough. You have to dig a little deeper to find out if your students are actually getting the material. It's perfectly appropriate to expect a teacher to do that very thing.

The only advice we can give you for demonstrating mastery in this domain, besides being prepared, is KNOW YOUR CONTENT. The more you know about a topic, the easier it is to respond to questions about that topic or see new ways of looking at that topic. You may have what you think is the perfect lesson in mind but find your students just aren't getting it. It's at that point you might very well have to think on your feet and approach the concept from a different angle, all the while being observed by someone typing down every word you say and pause you take. If you don't know your content, you may find yourself panicking because you only know one way of teaching that content. Equally disastrous would be a student catching you completely flat-footed with a question about something you should know. Sometimes, students will ask you obscure questions that aren't terrible significant or relevant to a lesson, but sometimes, they'll truly surprise you with an insightful one. The best way to be prepared for those kinds of questions and stay flexible in your lessons is to be an expert in your field.

The final domain in the Danielson model concerns Professional Responsibility, which covers the mundane tasks of maintaining attendance, grades, district and state paperwork, keeping your teacher webpage up to date, responding to parent phone calls/emails in a timely fashion, performing your duties around the school, attending in-service meeting and days, and generally "growing as a professional" and "showing professionalism." Meeting some of the components of this domain are extremely straightforward and, quite frankly, shouldn't even need to be listed. Your attendance record, for example, is a legal document and should be treated as such. It always amazed us how casual some teachers were about keeping accurate attendance. One of us knew a teacher who didn't even bother to do so. At the end of the semester, he simply borrowed someone else's attendance records and used them as his own! Chances are, though, you'll have to submit attendance every day, so getting a good evaluation in this category should be simple. The same should be true about grades, showing up on time for your duties, and attending required meetings.

It's in the realm of "growing as a professional" or "showing professionalism," though, it's tougher to get those higher evaluation marks. The obvious reason higher marks are more difficult to obtain is the vagueness of the language. You can ask an administrator what specific behaviors you have to exhibit to demonstrate "growing as a professional," but don't be surprised if that administrator fumbles about for an answer. Being a "professional" can mean different things to different people, so you may even find disagreement among the administrators at your school as to the true meaning. You may also find, as we did, some administrators don't have a hard-and-fast definition for "professionalism" and define it in different ways at different times, seemingly on a whim. In this case, our advice to you is to see if your evaluating administrator can give you some kind of documentation (i.e., handout or email) defining the components of this domain at the start of the semester. They may be unable or unwilling to provide you with such documentation, but it's at least worth a try to get it.

Aside from the Danielson model, another example of a popular teacher evaluation model is the Valued-Added Model (VAM). This model is based on the assumption you can figure out how much a student should "progress" during the course of the year based on how that student's done in the past and then evaluate the teacher on how well, or how little, the student actually progressed. For example, if you expect a student to progress from a sixth-grade reading level to a seventh-grade reading level during the course of seventh grade, the teachers in that school can be evaluated on how well that student progresses toward the seventh-grade reading level. Please note that in this model, it's not just the reading teacher who'd be evaluated, but all the student's teachers. The VAM score is not only a calculation of the progress a student makes in various subjects, it factors in such thing as school-wide scores on standardized tests, student attendance, and student behavior. In this model, then, a teacher's individual rating is tied to the collective rating of the faculty, as a whole. Our experience has been there's some degree of confusion or mystery about how the final VAM score is calculated, so our hope is your district gives you a clear idea of just how your VAM score is calculated.

Like the Danielson model, the VAM model may leave you with a number of questions and concerns. One of the validity issues with this type of evaluation is the prediction process, itself, which is the entire basis of the model. It disregards confounding variables, such as a student's prior knowledge of or interest in a topic. If a student doesn't do well in World

Cultures, for example, can we truly predict how that student will do in Civics? The two topics are completely different, of course, and it's quite possible to do well in one and not the other, but how would the equation change if the student has a strong interest in going into politics? Or how can you determine how well a student will do in Chemistry if that student did well in Biology? What if mom is a biologist and tutored the student at home? Can we automatically assume a person skilled in Biology will automatically be just as good at Chemistry? What happens if you get a student who scores 98 percent in a class one year and then 94 percent in another? Should the teacher get a lower rating since the student didn't "progress" as expected? As teachers, we were never told how "progress" was predicted or anything specific about how the data were compiled, so it's fair to question this critical underlying assumption of the model. How a student does in class is a multi-faceted process and can't be boiled down to simply what the teacher did. What happens inside the classroom is significant, of course, but there are also things within the student and outside the classroom that are quite relevant and should be considered.

This model is also based on the presupposition that the teacher is the only determining factor of whether the student will progress as expected. It's fair to ask how (or if) this model accounts for other variable that might affect a student's progress. For example, how can this model possibly control for things that happen in a student's life, such as a family member getting a serious illness, a friend dying, the beginning or ending of a romantic relationship, or any one of dozens of things that can affect a student's performance? Unless confounding variables are controlled somehow, how can we possibly be confident we're truly measuring the effect the teacher had on the student's progress? We have no answers to these questions but believe it's valid to ask them. We understand this model has the appeal of mathematical precision and accuracy, but unless we're confident this model truly measures what it claims to measure, we have our doubts as to its validity. If your district uses some type of VAM model, our advice is to try your best to understand how your overall score is calculated and do your best on the factors within your control.

How should we evaluate teachers?

Given the limitations of any teacher evaluation model, how can we begin to measure the qualities of a good teacher in a standardized fashion? The teacher obviously has an impact on student achievement, but is it possible to quantify how much impact? How confident could we be in such a measurement? Since teacher evaluations determine whether those teachers are retained or terminated, there should be a high level of confidence in those evaluations. If you look through various books, articles, or websites, there seems to be agreement that there are various aspects to what makes an effective teacher. These aspects include: what the teacher does before the students arrive for class, how the lesson is conducted, how the teacher interacts with students, what happens after the lesson, the teacher's responsibilities in helping the school run well, and how the teacher interacts with other adults (i.e., other staff members, administrators, and parents). It's critical to know, then, what makes a teacher "effective" at these things and how is that effectiveness measured.

As a starting point, we assume everyone would agree any evaluation for teachers should be fair, reliable, and valid. By "fair," we mean any evaluation system should be transparent enough so the teachers know what they need to do for high scores and that those high scores should actually be attainable. Besides benefiting the teachers, a fair system is desirable for the district since any employer would want employees to know ahead of time what the expectations are and how to meet them. By "reliable," we mean evaluation results are consistent and make allowances for the biases and personal preferences of the evaluators. For example, if three administrators evaluate the same teacher at the same time, all three of their evaluations should be virtually the same. Besides fairness and reliability, though, any assessment of teacher performance should also have validity. By "validity," we simply mean you're measuring what you say you're measuring. Complicating the process somewhat is the possibility of having a reliable measurement that's invalid. For example, if you had a scale that you set to be consistently thirty pounds too heavy and weigh something 1000 times and come up with the exact same weight, you'd probably feel pretty comfortable in saying the scale is reliable. The fact that each measurement is thirty pounds heavier than it should be, though, demonstrates the scale's measurements lack validity.

Concluding thoughts

Regardless of the evaluation system you find yourself under, you can be pretty sure it'll have shortcomings and you'll probably never be able to meet the top standard. In teacher evaluation, our experience has been that they continue to move the goalposts. In other words, the top score continues to get harder and harder to achieve, if it can even be achieved at all. If you are highly conscientious person, you'll probably be bothered by that fact, but don't take it as some kind of personal shortcoming. As cynical as it sounds, part of the reason why administrators evaluate teachers in the first place is to cover their own behinds. If they give you the highest marks as a teacher and then you somehow don't live up to those marks, it reflects badly on them, so they have an incentive to knock you down a peg in your score. Once again, don't take it personally but see it as simply a function of the evaluation system itself.

Some people may balk at our claim about teacher evaluation, but can you name any teacher role models? You may have some teachers who come to mind immediately, but ask yourself, can their efforts be duplicated by others or is what they do peculiar to their personality or situation? For example, if you have a high school science teacher who's set up a collaborative lab program with a local university, that's a wonderful thing, but can it be duplicated by other teachers? How can an Algebra teacher, an English teacher, or U.S. History teacher have a collaborative lab with a local university? They may be able to think of some kind of program, but will it get the approval of administration and parents? It isn't easy to duplicate unique successes, and at times it's impossible. Until examples are given of "ordinary" teachers meeting impossible standards, we'll stick to our claim that you're never really meant to reach the highest score on a teacher evaluation. Our belief is at some point a teacher is good enough and doesn't have to continually strive for perfection they, and perhaps no one else, can ever attain.

If you're still skeptical of our claim, look up examples of top ten teachers or great teachers. Are there any more recent than Jesus, Buddha, and Kong Qiu (Confucius)? Perhaps they exist, but we have never had any administrator give us an example of a living teacher we could model ourselves on. Let's assume, though, you find current examples of teachers who're recognized as "great." Are these individuals being lauded for teaching their actual subject areas, or are they being lauded for something else above and beyond what they're supposed to be teaching? Is it clear what criteria are used to demonstrate these are great teachers? Is there a way to tell a "great" teacher from a "good" teacher? If they don't provide any way of measuring great, then it's just a subjective distinction. If you're still doubtful about our claim, just use an example from another field. Compare the way teachers are ranked, say, to how top chefs are ranked. You can probably call to mind a great chef who could serve as an example to other chefs, but we are betting you could not do the same thing for a great teacher. The problem ultimately comes down to the fact that it's devilishly hard to measure all, or even most, of the elements that go into great teaching.

Are we saying, then, we should just throw up our hands and give up on evaluating teachers, then? Of course we aren't. A goal for any teacher evaluation system should be to develop and retain competent teachers in order to maximize student learning, but that doesn't mean you should constantly fall short of some never-defined ideal. You'll always have something to work on, but "you've never arrived" is quite different from "you're never good enough." An evaluation system should challenge teachers to think about if and how they can get better, but it should also set realistic and attainable standards and give teachers a sense they're constantly growing in their job. Our experience has been that current evaluation systems for teachers focus more on finding fault than fostering improvement. There's nothing easier than criticizing someone for not being perfect. It's lazy, it also doesn't take any particular skill or knowledge, and it's ultimately demoralizing to the staff. Our hope is that teacher evaluation continues to be examined and developed, but you should be aware it has a long way to go if you're choosing teaching as your career.

Chapter 10

"THE SYSTEM IS BROKEN!"

Introduction

One teacher was in an afterschool meeting with an administrator and a small group of colleagues tasked with "reimagining the high school experience." Since no one knew exactly what they were being asked to do, including the administrator, the meeting quickly degenerated into educational buzzwords and clichés. The one phrase that stuck out, though, was the administrator repeatedly exclaiming, "The system is broken!" After hearing that cliché for the third time, the teacher asked, "As compared to what?" The administrator gave a puzzled look, so the teacher continued, "You keep saying the system is broken, so you must have some idea of what 'fixed' looks like. What does fixed look like?" The administrator ignored the question, the meeting continued, and nothing of value came out of it. The following day, the teacher was called into an afterschool ambush meeting where the principal scolded him for asking questions in the previous day's meeting. When the teacher explained he was simply looking for a clarification of what the other administrator was saying, the principal made it very clear that asking questions was considered borderline harassment, and that he better not do it again.

These types of meetings probably happen all the time in schools around the country. It seems there's universal agreement that something's "wrong" with education and that something needs to be done to fix it, and we've certainly seen a variety of proposed solutions. None of these simplistic solutions, though, ever addressed the most significant and complicated problems facing education, and the fact that no one has stumbled upon the answer that will fix everything wrong with education tells us it's a multifaceted and complex problem. It's clear that pointing out the current system falls short of some vague notion of perfection isn't helpful and doesn't inform any kind of action, nor does using teachers as easy scapegoats. We don't claim to have discovered El Dorado or any other elusive and mysterious solution to education's woes, but we would like you to give you our perspective on a few of the issues surrounding education and give you some things to think about if you decide you're going to make teaching your lifelong pursuit.

A quick note on clarity and precision

Before getting into specifics about what may or may not be wrong with education, the issue of clarity must be addressed. Clarity is simply the idea that what you're saying is clear and thus interpreted the same way by everyone hearing you. If you say something like "the system is broken," the words "system" and "broken" can both be interpreted in many different ways, so they're lacking in clarity. Unless everyone is talking about the same thing, you'll get nowhere in terms of productive discussion. Unfortunately, in all our years of hearing talk about how the system needs to be fixed, no one has ever identified the problem they sought to address in terms that everyone could understand. There seemed to be a presupposition that everyone discussing an issue was fully versed in the background knowledge of the person speaking and how that person was framing the argument. You should never just assume people know what you mean by certain vague terms you use, so any productive discussion of education (or anything else, really) should begin with a common vocabulary and understanding of the context of any issue.

Closely related to the idea of clarity is precision in language. Typically, when people talk about education, they don't provide enough detail for everyone to clearly understand what they're trying to say. For example, we've heard numerous people say that the system needs to "change," with the unstated assumption that all change is good. Unless things are so bad that any change at all would be an improvement, a little bit more detail about the exact nature of the proposed change should be offered. If you go to the doctor, for example, and are told that a spot on your lung has changed, that's probably not good news and you'd certainly like to know something more specific. Since not all change is good change, then, you have to be detailed about the kind of change you're talking about. Unless everyone understands what you're trying to say in sufficient detail to understand it and comment on it, you can't move forward in any discussion.

Do we need more funding or more administrators?

While working at a rather affluent district, one of my students told me he was conducting a fundraiser for a local inner-city school. When I asked him why he was doing that, he looked very puzzled and said, "Well, they don't get the kind of money we do." When I told him they actually spent more money per pupil in that district than they did in ours, he looked completely taken back. I told him to look into it himself, and the next day he came in shaking his head and said, "You were right, they spend thousands of dollars more per student there than they do here." He still conducted his fundraiser, but his assumption about funding seems to be a common one: that inner-city schools are far less funded than suburban schools. Our experience has been the exact opposite. We can't make a blanket statement about every district, but it only takes a few minutes to find the spending per pupil of your local public school district, so making comparisons between and among districts is no great obstacle or mystery. We tell the story because one of the things we heard through our entire careers was that one of the things currently wrong with "the system" is a lack of funding. "We need more funding" has been a near-constant battle cry from teachers, administrators, and politicians. Despite hearing that plea from different people at different times, we've never heard anyone explain *why* the funding was needed. They might've outlined what they were going to do with the money and perhaps even given the name of a new program, but the assumption seemed to be the benefits of increased spending were self-evident. Someone would have an idea that sounded plausible, the idea would be funded, implemented, but then there'd be no real (if any) consideration of testing its effectiveness empirically. We, however, are operating under the assumption that the ultimate reason for more funding is improving student achievement in some measurable way.

Our further assumption is if you call yourself a professional and propose spending hundreds of thousands of the tax payers' dollars, you better have more than a hunch that something sounds good and might work. Any proposed increase in funding should be scrutinized with some basic questions. Will this increase in funding lead to greater student achievement? What evidence will there be to prove that it was the increased funding that led to the improvement in student achievement and not some other factor(s)? What problem or educational shortcoming, specifically, will be solved by more money? How much more money is necessary? What evidence is there that a specific amount of money would solve the problem? Are we spending the money we currently have efficiently? Our position is that since lower-income people or people on fixed incomes might very well be taxed out of their homes by bloated education budgets, the burden of proof is on the school board to *prove* why the increased spending is necessary.

Another popular argument we heard was that a way to fix "the system" was to hire more administrators. Once again, on some level it seems reasonable to assume more administrators would in some way help the education process, but just because something sounds plausible doesn't make it so. It's fair to ask a few basic questions before tax payer dollars are spent on creating a new position. What sort of administrator should be hired? Is it the case this person will help improve educational outcomes for students, or would this person perform some other function? How can we test to see if adding such an administrator leads to better student outcomes? Like any organization, the school district will absorb a new administrator and find something for that person to do, but is it truly worth the money to have such a person? Everyone who works in the school district should be able to justify his or her job, and administrators are no different. All of this is not to deny more administrators may be needed in various districts but merely to point out there should be hard evidence to justify the hiring of such people in order to help "fix" education.

Are the teachers the problem?

Perhaps the most frequently cited fix for "the system" we heard during our careers was weeding out the bad teachers. We should all certainly begin with several points of agreement when it comes to teachers. First is the recognition that there are "bad" teachers out there, and they should either be improved or removed from the classroom. Right away, though, we have to define specifically what a "bad" teacher is. It's certainly appropriate and desirable to evaluate teachers for the benefit of the students, taxpayers, the district, and other teachers, but we should all agree that such a process be transparent and fair for the benefit of all parties involved. After all, recruiting and retaining quality teachers would be far more difficult in a district with a reputation for an unfair or vindictive evaluation process. Before we delve into the specifics of teacher evaluation today, it's helpful to establish a point of comparison from the past.

The first thing we want to note is that how teachers are evaluated changed drastically during our careers. When we first started teaching in the early 1990s, the teacher evaluation process was, admittedly, far too easy on teachers. A typical observation consisted of an administrator walking into the classroom, staying for about ten minutes, and then leaving. Within a few days, you'd get a note in your mailbox saying something like, "You did a great job the other day," and that was it. Normally, you'd get two such observations a year, although sometimes only one, and then you received the coveted "Satisfactory" rating. In order to receive an "Unsatisfactory" rating, more of a process was required, but we can't recall any colleague of ours receiving such a rating, though certainly a couple of them probably should have. It was clear at that time teachers were evaluated on how they prepared for and presented the lesson, with an emphasis on lesson presentation. Such an approach would be completely alien to a teacher today and, admittedly, the old system certainly was inadequate for evaluating teachers.

In the early 2000s, there was a seismic shift in evaluating teachers that focused not on what the teacher was doing, but on what the students were doing. We were told not to be "the sage on the stage, but the guide on the side." In order to get the highest evaluation under the new system, the students in your class now had to be teaching themselves and their fellow students. The assumption seemingly was that the teacher, mainly acting as an observer, needed only to point the knowledge-thirsty scholars in the right direction and somehow the magical process of education would occur. If a group of fifteen-year-olds weren't discussing and discovering the wonders of the plant cell, then it was obviously the teacher's fault and nothing else. Forgive our obvious skepticism, but anyone who's been a student realizes that such expectations are laughable for the average class. Students certainly tutor each other and can be of huge benefit, make no mistake, but expecting the students to drive all learning is a bridge too far.

This shifting model of teacher evaluation seemed to come from the corresponding movement to seeing education as a kind of business. The assumption was that it's both possible and desirable to collect some form of "data" on education that could then drive an evaluation process of both the teacher and the school. This new pseudo-business model focused on "producing results" as if teachers were meeting a monthly sales quota. Admittedly, the model definitely did, and does, have an appeal. During the course of our careers, we heard several people say, "I'm responsible for the product I produce, so teachers should be responsible for the product they produce." The unstated conclusion was since, nationally, students weren't doing as well as desired, the teachers were the breakdown in the system. Focus on making or getting better teachers, and the problem would be solved. It sounds perfectly reasonable and has the allure of being a simplistic, satisfying explanation for the topic, but it's an overly simplistic view, as if teachers were producing widgets instead of dealing with living, breathing students. Hand in hand with this new business model approach was the standardized test taking center stage, almost to the exclusion of anything else. Standardized testing has its place, of course, but a test score certainly doesn't tell you the whole story about an individual child. It's far more informative to have teachers who are quite familiar with the student's day-to-day work giving that student a final evaluation. Take standardized test scores seriously, but realize they only represent a small sample of a student's overall progress in a subject. Teachers should certainly be evaluated in terms of their professionalism, expertise in their field, and how well they deal with children, but to think that's the only problem with education is simply picking on the lowest hanging fruit.

Let's do a little thought exercise to show how complex education gets and how inappropriate it is to evaluate teachers as being the sole determinant of a student's grade. Do teachers raise their students, or is it the parent(s)? Do teachers live with their students every day? Do teachers have as much influence over children as their siblings and peers do, especially during the teenage years? Do teachers have any real control over if the child does homework or if the child goes to bed early enough to get proper rest? Is it the teacher who's texting a student at 2:30 a.m. to chat or play an online video game? Is it the teacher who decides he "isn't good at math" and doesn't even try? Is it right to hold teachers responsible as the only possible factor determining a student's grade? Realistically, teachers see a student perhaps forty-five minutes a day, five days a week, at most.

The time spent in actual one-on-one conversation is far less than that. The amount of actual influence a teacher has over a student's grade is part of an incredibly complex equation, with the individual factors of that equation varying from student to student. You could have the best parents and the best teacher in the world, but that in no way guarantees a particular student will do well in a given class. There are far too many variables involved to make simplistic judgments about teachers, however emotionally satisfying drawing such judgments may be.

It's also important to make a number of distinctions when evaluating teachers in order to get an even more sophisticated view of the process. The first distinction you should make is between those who major in Education as an undergraduate degree and those who major in a specific subject, such as History, and then go on to get their teaching certificate. It's fair to ask if an Education major assigned to teach a History class has as much knowledge of the field as someone who majored in History. Verifying the expertise of teachers is certainly a start in teacher evaluation, and no one should have a problem with more rigorous academic tests before teachers can teach their given subjects or having veteran teachers retest in their given subjects. Getting a teacher with in-depth knowledge of a subject area is certainly desirable, but doing so will not magically solve all the issues with education, given the number of variables involved. Our suspicion is retesting teachers on their subject would have very little impact at all. It is a start, however, in restoring the public's confidence in the competence of their local teachers.

Another distinction to make among teachers, and one far more complex to measure, is where the teacher is most effective. The most obvious delineation to make here is between Elementary teachers and Secondary (high school) teachers. Some people are simply better suited to dealing with younger children than others, and these are the folks who gravitate naturally to the elementary schools, which is altogether desirable. You could very well have a wonderful high school teacher who'd be utterly ineffective teaching very young children. It's also the case that some teachers have a gift for teaching higher-achieving students. Other teachers may have a gift for teaching lower-achieving students who perhaps have more emotional needs that have to be met before they can focus on the academics. It's quite possible to move an AP Calculus teacher from a high-performing district to a lower-achieving school and find that teacher is completely ineffective. Was the teacher great in one school and then not the other? Was the teacher always bad and that fact was just covered up by the types of students involved? How confident are we in making such conclusions? We suspect you could take the faculty from a low-achieving school, move it to a high-achieving school, and the students would do just as well. Conversely, we also suspect you could take the faculty from a high-achieving school, move it to a low-achieving school, and the students would do just as badly. How, then, can we determine which grade level or level of achievement each teacher is best suited for? Currently, teachers sort themselves into Elementary and Secondary teachers by choosing their own given certifications. Beyond that, though, a teacher's schedule is determined by someone else. Is that the most effective way? Can we ascertain whether or not the teacher is in the right place? Should that ninth-grade Civics teacher actually be teaching AP U.S. Government and Politics? Frankly, we have no answers to these questions. We present them simply to give some small insight into the complexities of evaluating teachers, in general.

A final consideration is although certain qualities of an effective teacher are easy to measure reliably and validly, such as whether or not a lesson plan meets a list of specific criteria, there are some very significant qualities of an effective teacher that are extremely difficult, if not impossible, to measure. For example, it seems reasonable to assume a teacher should have some degree of empathy, but can empathy be measured in a meaningful way when it comes to evaluating a teacher? Psychological testing of prospective teachers, besides having serious legal and moral issues surrounding it, was not something we experienced, but would it be helpful even if a district could do it? Who would decide how much "empathy" a teacher should have? What level of empathy, precisely, does an effective teacher have, and what's the evidence that such a level of specific empathy leads to higher student achievement? Is there evidence that teachers who are, say, more empathetic than 75 percent of the general population account for increased student achievement? It has to be a measurable score so you can rank teachers by their score. Given the realities of teacher shortages, especially in the STEM fields, would it be wise to automatically disqualify a teacher for being a point or two shy of your empathy cutoff? The point of this thought exercise is not to advocate for evaluating teachers for their empathy but to demonstrate how complicated it can get determining a single desirable quality of a teacher. How complicated it is to measure such a quality shouldn't necessarily determine whether that quality is measured, but it should provoke serious and deep thought about whether it is worth the time and expense to do so.

Should parents get more involved?

We've also heard it said one of the things wrong with education is that parents aren't involved enough with the curriculum. Since the COVID lockdowns, it seems parents are more involved and more aware of what's being taught in the schools via online lessons than ever before. The very first thing we'd like to stress is that you shouldn't be hiding anything you teach in your classroom from administrators, parents, or the taxpayers. Everything you teach should relate to state and/or district standards for education, and you should be able to justify everything that's taught in any lesson. In these politically charged times, in particular, don't be surprised at all if some students are paying attention to everything you say, trying to glean your political biases or personal worldview. Parents, too, may be paying attention to everything you say for the same reason. Nothing like that should make you nervous or intimidate you. If you follow the district-approved curriculum and stick to your subject area, you should be fine. Parents taking a greater interest in their children's education should make your job easier, in the long run, because most of them will support what you do in class and have the best interest of their children in mind. You, also, have the best interest of the children in mind, so your priorities and the parent's priorities should generally coincide.

That being said, we need to be more specific here about parental involvement because some hard questions present themselves immediately: what exactly does it mean for parents to get "more involved?" How much, exactly, and in what manner should parents "get involved?" What's the evidence this involvement would work? The assumption with this approach seems to be that more parental involvement will lead to better curriculum and increased student achievement (assuming student achievement is our ultimate goal), but how can we test that assumption? In terms of what's actually taught in the classroom, to what extent should the parents decide what the best curriculum is? Are they best qualified to decide issues of curriculum, or should such decisions be left to administrators or teachers? Even if parents aren't the best judges of curriculum, they are the ones footing the bill and therefore should have some sort of voice. If it's to be a collaborative effort among parents and school officials, how can differences among parents be resolved? How do we guard against parents with political agendas? All these questions are beyond a classroom teacher's authority to decide, of course, but you should be aware that platitudes such as "we need more parent involvement" are thrown around in faculty meetings as if they're in some way insightful or new. If your school truly believes a lack of parental involvement is what's wrong with education and is serious about getting the parents more involved, that's great, but we suggest you think about some of the questions we've posed before blindly accepting that the magical cure for education's woes has been discovered.

Are teaching methods the problem?

Speaking of magical cures, seemingly every year during our careers we heard of a new initiative, program, or set of educational terms that was to act as just such a cure. Our suspicion is that your experience will be similar if you decide to go into teaching. Unfortunately, despite these new initiatives being rolled out with great enthusiasm, it was never explained to us what specific problem these initiatives were addressing and how exactly they would improve anything. At the risk of sounding defeated, our view is there is no magical cure for all that is wrong with education and that we waste time and effort looking for such a thing, but administrators will no doubt keep trying. Several of the initiatives presented to us centered around the idea of standardization, so it's fair to ask if standardizing instruction and testing is a potential cure for education's woes.

An early initiative related to standardization, and one that's still around, is the concept of standards-based education. It was originally called "Outcomes Based Education," but that term quickly became unpopular politically, so it was changed. Don't be confused if someone says "outcomes" or "standards," that person is probably using those terms interchangeably. Standards-based education is simply the idea that student achievement should be measured against a fixed standard, and not against everyone else in the class. For example, students used to be graded along a normal distribution or "bell curve," which meant they were being compared to how others did in the class. One of us was even asked in an interview if we believed student grades should always fall into a "bell curve" with most students getting "Cs." In standards-based education, student performance is compared to a fixed standard. In such a system, it's possible for all students to earn an "A" as long as they meet the standard. For example, if you think of a driver's exam, you're thinking of a standards-based situation. Each person taking the test is judged on driving skill, and not by how well that person compares to other people who've taken the test. There's a list of specific demonstrable behaviors each person must exhibit in order to be considered proficient.

One of the teachers we knew, for example, taught carpentry and used the carpenters' apprenticeship test as his final exam.

Standard-based education, assuming the standards are appropriate, can be of great benefit to both the students and the teachers. For example, students (and parents) will know ahead of time what they need to do to demonstrate mastery of a subject or skill and will understand how they fell short if that standard isn't reached. Having clear standards also helps focus the efforts of the teacher and takes away much of the guess work that can plague a first or second-year teacher, in particular. All students meeting that standard, for example, will have a basic grasp of the most important ideas and skills of a given topic, so the teacher will be able to make informed decisions about whether it's time to move on to a new topic or if a topic needs to be revisited. Well-defined state standards would also aid the teacher in communicating with parents and addressing parent concerns.

A potential shortcoming of standards-based education, and a highly significant one, is which standards are chosen and how those standards are written. Our experience was the state created the standards without any input from local teachers or parents. It was never clear who wrote the standards, what qualified them to do so, or how those standards could be challenged or changed. In our opinion, standards for a subject should have come out of a transparent process that focused on consensus, but we were never sure who was involved in choosing the standards. An even bigger shortcoming we found, though, was the vagueness in language of too many of the standards. As teachers, we weren't sure how each standard could be met, and the lack of clarity rendered too many of them of no value in the classroom. We've always been of the opinion that if state standards are so important, and they are, they should be written in language students can understand. Until such time standards are clear and meaningful to students, we don't see them solving education's woes.

Related to the movement towards standards-based education was a new emphasis on standardized testing. Standardized testing is certainly something you experienced as a student and will encounter as a teacher, so you should also consider its pros and cons. The impetus behind standardized testing was that it allowed parents, teachers, and administrators to compare apples to apples across the district, state, and even the nation. That is to say the performance of an individual school could be compared to schools as a whole, something that couldn't be done fairly before these tests were implemented. In theory, teachers and school districts could then be evaluated based on the standardized test scores of their students. Assuming the test focuses on the most significant concepts of a discipline, a standardized test also focuses the efforts of teachers by allowing them to "teach to the test." And finally, like standards-based education, proficiency on a standardized test demonstrates a student has achieved an acceptable level of knowledge and skill within an academic discipline. Standardized tests are most likely here to stay, so you shouldn't be intimidated by them and should be able to justify their proper use.

As with any other form of testing, though, there are potential shortcomings of standardized testing, as well. In our own state, for example, the first time the Biology test was given it didn't "count" but was merely being used as a baseline measurement. The students were aware the test didn't mean anything to their grade or advancement, so some of them didn't even bother taking it. Even when standardized tests did determine whether or not a student would pass a particular subject, we still had students who simply threw the test on the floor, put their heads down, and refused to take it. That rendered any baseline measurement of the test completely invalid, of course. Another real issue we ran into was the lack of validity of some tests. Some of our students failed the Biology test, for example, not because of their lack of subject knowledge but because their reading level was so low they couldn't understand the questions. Other students were also intimidated by the essay section and didn't even try. All of this isn't to condemn standardized tests but to simply make you aware of the potential pitfalls of drawing quick conclusions without fully understanding the context in which the scores were derived.

A more recent proposed solution to education's shortcomings is programmed curriculum. This initiative arose out of the desire to standardize not only what is taught, but also *how* it's taught. We've probably all experienced classes where one teacher is a month or two behind another teacher teaching the same subject or one teacher is a "tough" grader. If two teachers are teaching the same class and, presumably, the same curriculum, it isn't desirable to have them teaching at wildly different paces or grading in substantially different ways. A programmed curriculum is designed to guard again such variations in teaching by providing a prepackaged course of study given to each teacher that includes a daily script of want to teach and how to teach it. Assuming teachers follow the curriculum, students taking the same courses should have similar experiences.

One benefit of such a curriculum is it ensures each student will be exposed to a common core of knowledge, vocabulary, and thinking on a subject. In theory, it removes the concern that some students will lack some of the fundamental information of a subject that other students are being taught. A related benefit is all students will cover material necessary to do well on a standardized test. Since standardized tests are of increasing importance in evaluating districts, it's important for students to do well on them. This standardized instruction also provides benefit if a student transfers from one school in the district to the other. The student won't be behind the other students, which is quite desirable in a district that has a lot of transient students. Finally, it also, in theory, protects against bad teachers since every teacher will be given a step-by-step instruction guide on what to teach, when to teach it, and how to teach it.

A major shortcoming of this approach, though, is since you're pretty much reading a script every day, it doesn't allow for variability in student learning. If a student or class is struggling with a concept, you won't have time to reteach that concept because then you'll fall behind schedule. It also doesn't take into account the normal interruptions of a school day and school week. One poorly timed fire drill can throw your entire week's schedule off kilter and leave you scrambling for a way to make up for it. That kind of inflexibility in a curriculum is a major handicap, in our opinion. Teachers must always be in tune with the needs of their students and can't be bound to a curriculum that simply crunches along at a particular pace, students be damned. A teacher's purpose is to serve the needs of the students, not some arbitrary timeframe. Finally, there's also a danger a programed curriculum can actually protect ineffective teachers, as well, because they're given a strict script on how to run the lesson. Even if a poor teacher was incapable of teaching a lesson in a different way, it doesn't matter because a programed curriculum doesn't allow for the lesson to be retaught, anyway. Supporters of programmed curriculum would probably be livid at our characterization and point out there certainly *is* flexibility in the curriculum and that teachers are given time to reteach. We were told it was okay to be a day ahead or a day behind, that's true, but there was also the unstated but clear threat you better not deviate from the curriculum. If an administrator came to observe you on a Tuesday and you were still covering Monday's material, they were going to call you on it.

A final initiative we wanted to highlight, and also one with which you're no doubt familiar, is the idea of cooperative learning. In a cooperative learning classroom, students work together in small groups and "teach themselves" the material. The teacher's role is to collect the materials necessary for the lesson, instruct the students on how to begin the learning process, and then the students do the majority of the work on their own, with the teacher there to answer any questions that might arise. For example, a class might be broken into four groups to learn about four programs of the New Deal of the 1930s. Each group would become the "experts" on their particular program and be responsible for teaching the rest of the class about their particular

New Deal program. Students within each group would have a well-defined role, such as facilitator or recorder, to help guard against social loafing.

One of the strengths of this approach is that, since students are taking a more active role in their own learning, they learn the material in greater depth. As we were told, "You'll be working less, the kids will be working more." It's also assumed the material is more memorable for them since they're the ones doing the learning and not passively receiving information via lecture or a reading. Since they're responsible for teaching the material to others, it's also hoped the students will put more thought into what the most significant parts of the learning are. And finally, since other students may ask questions about their topics, it's hoped students will be motivated to know the topic well enough to respond.

Unfortunately, our experience with cooperative learning was that it was based on some false premises. First of all, we never ran into an entire group of students who were so highly motivated that they were willing to teach themselves and others. Teaching is a lot of work, and we're run into very few students who actually relished that work. This approach also assumes people who aren't content experts will pick out the most significant ideas to cover and cover those ideas in an appropriate depth. The argument can be made that the whole point of the assignment is to make them content experts, but expecting students to gain the knowledge and skill of a teacher is simply unfair and unrealistic. Arguments such as these stem from the assumption anyone can teach, which is an assumption we reject. Part of being a teacher is being a content expert, but another part of being a teacher is being a professional speaker. We certainly shouldn't expect students to be both.

Is merit pay the answer?

A final way we've heard to "fix" the "system" is merit pay for teachers. Merit pay is based on the assumption teachers will "work harder" if it means more money for them. Self-interest is certainly a good and reliable motivating factor for people and it seems reasonable to assume that a more motivated or enthusiastic teacher would be more effective, but do we *know* that or are we just guessing? What does "working harder" or being "more motivated" look like, specifically, in terms of teachers? What behaviors are affected? What would teachers do under a merit pay system that they aren't currently doing? What's the evidence that merit pay for teachers increases certain behaviors? How can we test this theory? Even if it turns out teacher merit pay benefits students, we still aren't done. What kind of financial incentive would it take to achieve the maximum level of motivation in the most cost-effective way (we would need a specific dollar amount and some idea of how confident we are that dollar amount is correct)? All of these questions, and no doubt others we haven't identified, should be addressed before a merit pay system could be implemented.

Another thing to consider when discussing merit pay is not everybody is equally motivated by money, so a one-size-fits-all approach is suspect from the very beginning. We don't know for a fact that financial incentives are the primary motivating factor for people who go into teaching, so is there some other way we can achieve better student results besides bigger pay checks for "good" teachers? How can you measure a teacher who inspires you or gives you a new perspective on life? Some of the most valuable lessons we can learn in school may have nothing to do with the subject matter. Are we to believe because things can't be measured directly that they're not worthwhile or valuable? It's also the case with complicated issues more than one factor has to be considered. There are a number of questions, then, that need to be addressed empirically before we can start drawing conclusions about merit pay as a solution.

Let's begin with the teacher's behavior that will presumably be affected by merit pay. In order to simplify things, let's ignore the influence of parents, student peers, and the students themselves and focus solely on teacher behavior both in and outside of the classroom. There are three general parts to teaching any lesson: preparation, execution, and evaluation of the lesson's effectiveness. Which one of these aspects would be affected by merit pay? Any teacher worth his or her salt would be well prepared for class, so should taxpayers be expected to pay extra for something a teacher should be doing anyway? We think not. In terms of the execution of the lesson, we would need to know exactly how merit pay would make a teacher more effective. And once again, we run into the issue of shouldn't we expect teachers to conduct their lessons properly as part of their job and not something extra? In terms of the evaluation of the lesson, that simply deals with knowing whether or not the students truly learned what they were supposed to learn or if the lesson needs to be changed for future classes. How, exactly, would merit pay make that process better?

Another consideration before implementing merit pay is how we determine which teachers deserve it. One basis we've heard has been to base merit pay on either the number of students who get A's or on student satisfaction surveys. Both of those solutions have the same problem, though. If a teacher's salary is based on the number of A's given, that provides an incentive for teachers to give easy A's. If a teacher's salary is based on the satisfaction of students, once again, giving out easy A's would fit the bill. You may be thinking administrators could guard against such behavior, but we doubt very much that would happen. In our careers, we never heard of any teacher being criticized for being too easy on students or giving out too many A's. Administrators would also be afraid to push back against easy grades for fear of upsetting the parents.

A final consideration about merit pay is the difficulty in applying it across different disciplines. Immediately, we run into complexity because not all subjects require the same amount of preparation. In math, unit plans and lesson plans are typically pretty straightforward, so we wouldn't expect someone teaching Algebra I to have to go through the same preparation as a Chemistry teacher who's about to conduct a lab. Labs have to be set up ahead of time and taken down, of course, so the level of preparation is different than it is in the typical math class. Would the Algebra teacher be more motivated to prepare a lesson knowing that a well-prepared lesson would mean more money? What about the Chemistry teacher? Should the Chemistry teacher get higher pay since the preparation is more complex and time-consuming? What if we're dealing with a class that doesn't have a standardized test associated with it, such as Ceramics? Should we say a Ceramics teacher shouldn't qualify for merit pay? If so, how is that equitable? Should we then rank teachers in their order of importance, with Math or Science teachers being at the top and Art and Music teachers being at the bottom?

Can we just simplify the issue and base merit pay on student surveys? The idea of students evaluating their teachers has gained a good deal of traction, and it doesn't look like the practice is going away anytime soon. Some administrators who teach college courses actually have their students fill out evaluations at the end of every lesson! We're highly skeptical of such evaluations because students are in no way qualified to evaluate the quality of a teacher. If you asked the typical student to articulate the qualities of a good teacher, you'd probably get things like, "they're nice" or something similar. There are also too many extraneous factors that could affect their rating. For example, if they like the teacher, they're going to give the teacher higher ratings regardless of that person's ability. If the teacher is "too hard," then they're going to give that teacher lower ratings. Ratings wouldn't be valid or reliable, and students might not even take them seriously. We also find it rather insulting that administrators trust students to rate their teachers but don't trust teachers to evaluate their administrators.

Concluding thoughts

Clearly, there isn't a shortage of ideas about how to improve education, and new and revised solutions will no doubt continue to be advanced during your career, whether they focus on parents, administrators, teachers, or students. We certainly haven't given you an exhaustive list of all the proposed solutions for increasing student outcomes, but we hope our examples help you make some sense of things. There are certainly a lot more approaches out there, including personalized or individualized learning, differentiated learning, and so forth. It isn't within the scope of this book to go through each and every one of them, but a common theme among them is the idea it's possible to improve educational outcomes without being terribly clear about how to do so. If nothing else, it's our hope our experiences will help you make sense of these new approaches and not feel so bad if they don't seem to make sense.

Chapter 11

CAN EDUCATION
BE "FIXED?"

Introduction

If you do make that final decision to become a teacher, you would do well to have some idea of what a "fixed" education system looks like because you'll certainly be part of that system. In addition to giving you practical things to focus on in your teaching, knowing what "fixed" looks like will also provide a philosophical justification and focus for your instruction, both in the beginning and throughout your career. Once again, we don't claim to have all the answers but do believe our experience will give you some things to consider before you actually take your place in the classroom. An overarching piece of advice we would give you is don't waste time chasing an idealized world or a perfect solution. There are real limitations on what any education system or teacher can do, so our focus should be on doing the best we can with the limited resources available. Kicking ourselves or other teachers because we've fallen short of some unachievable notion of perfection isn't helpful to anyone involved. We should certainly always be on the lookout for better ways of teaching our students, without question, but we must also keep in mind that education is a multi-faceted and complex process.

So, how should we begin thinking about "fixing" the "system?" We think it's most helpful to look at education's problems in terms of the individuals involved, and not some set of shadowy, undefinable forces such as "society." Such thinking isn't specific enough to inform any kind of insight or potential action. Our focus, then, should be on the students, parents, administrators, and teachers. We should have both a clear idea of what we want an "educated" student to look like and also how the other people involved can help achieve that goal. Further, we also need to be realistic and acknowledge certain people and circumstances are both within our control and beyond our control. We should do what we can to produce the best students possible while realizing certain circumstances and people will actively work against that goal. We don't want to be pessimistic and say education can't be improved, but we also can't be unsophisticated and think it'll be easy (or even possible, in some cases).

What do we want educated students to look like?

Throughout our careers, we've heard many discussions about how teachers are falling short in educating students and how teachers might improve their instruction and evaluation of students, which is appropriate, but we believe the first place to start when examining education is our goals for the students. What do we want our children to look like once they've been properly educated? Without specific goals in mind, the whole educational approach would be disjointed and likely unsuccessful. What are some of those goals? There's room for discussion and debate, but at a minimum we believe students should think, write, and speak clearly to the best of their ability. There's complexity here, of course. Students should have a common core of knowledge in various subjects in order to understand and communicate with each other. Students should be able to clearly explain what it is they believe and why. Their beliefs should be based on evidence, relevant experience, and consideration of a variety of viewpoints, as opposed to mere opinion or fear. We believe it's desirable for students to have a healthy sense of skepticism, as well. By skepticism, we mean they don't believe the first thing they hear without considering other viewpoints and evidence. Skepticism does not mean cynicism, or that they simply take the easy way out and reject all ideas without examining them. The last thing any of us wants is students who are completely simpleminded and believe the first thing they're told without considering any other way of looking at the topic.

If you think about it, we want our students to be thinkers and life-long learners. Given the complexity of the world, we can look at "thinkers" as those who impose order on chaos. They're people who recognize they don't know everything and are willing to keep learning in an ever-changing world. As adults, we want our former students to adapt to new situations. We want them to be able to identify the most important issues of their lives, understand them in depth, and have a solid background in a range of different disciplines. It's also important they be able to distinguish fact from opinion and be able to see through any information that's manipulating them or leading them to a pre-determined conclusion. There's no shortage of people in this world who want to tell other people what to think, so it's reasonable for teachers to expect their former students to resist jumping to quick conclusions before all the facts are examined.

Arriving at this goal of creating critical thinkers and lifelong learners clearly opens up a number of questions about their actual instruction during school, and we believe that's a good thing. We need to start with what kind of classroom experiences we want our kids to have in order to achieve our larger goals for them (whatever we decide those goals are). And make no mistake, if we did consider the ultimate goals of education first, we'd definitely run into pushback from some people. For example, we certainly wouldn't want students taking the path of least resistance in order to get some arbitrary grade, but rather, we'd want them developing some kind of work ethic and carry knowledge away from each class. There are parents and administrators, though, who would clearly fight against such an approach for various reasons. As a teacher, realize you may be able to do little or nothing in the face of such resistance. You will also encounter resistance from students. We don't want our students to be passive, expecting to have conclusions prepackaged for them, but that's exactly what many of them want. As teachers, we could (and often do) fight against the tide and push for what's best for our students in the long run, but students and other adults often don't look at things in the long run and truly do want the path of least resistance. Given that reality, the best we can do is make the case for those things that are the most beneficial for students in the long run while realizing our efforts will be in vain a lot of the time. As hard as you try or as much as you care, some kids, for whatever reason, will never reach their full potential. As teachers, we must work within the reality that there are some things within our control and some things without. Knowing the difference between them, though frustrating at times, will help you cope better with the limitations of teaching.

What can teachers control?

Despite those things outside of our control, there are at least certain basic expectations about teachers within our control. For example, one of the things clearly within our control is the basic academic standards for teachers. Is it the case higher standardized test scores would give us more qualified teachers? Should teacher certification programs include more classes or more time spent in an actual classroom? Are there ways to identify more effective teachers before they actually make it into the classroom? All of these issues can be explored and render hard data, but is there any motivation to do so? Other elements of teachers clearly don't lend themselves to hard data but are equally important. For example, how can we measure a teacher helping someone become a better student or look at the world in a different way? How can we properly evaluate a teacher who inspires a student to pursue a field of study that eventually becomes that student's career? One of us, for example, had two former students, both Ivy Leaguers, tell us we were the reason they became teachers. Such influence is highly impactful, of course, but we must recognize that a teacher's influence can never be fully measured or controlled.

Another aspect of teaching, and one within our control as teachers, is our individual effort and attitude. Although it may not change the system dramatically, all teachers should put forth maximum effort in their job. A fundamental area of knowledge is content knowledge, and there should be no question that teachers know their content. Throughout your career, you should work on your weaknesses and not just teach information you know. Sadly, the U.S. History teachers we had as students were a notorious example of lazy teachers. They taught the American Revolution, skipped to the Civil War, and then skipped to World War II. If you find yourself teaching a subject and are tempted to skip over the parts you don't know, don't! Study that area until you're comfortable with it. Maybe even challenge yourself to turn something you don't know well into one of your strengths. Learning something new about your subject should also help keep you motivated and excited about your subject, which is a reasonable expectation for any teacher. Do everything you can to relate content you're teaching to the students' lives. You should constantly be thinking of ways to do that throughout the year. No one should have to motivate you or get you enthusiastic about your subject, that's your job. If you can't get excited about what you're teaching, then how can you expect the kids to buy into it as something worthwhile? Tell your students something new about your subject you've only just learned, let them see you reading an article or book to expand your knowledge, let them know your subject is alive and interesting. Students should see you demonstrate the concept of being a lifelong learner. You can *tell* them they should continue to learn after they leave your class, but that's not nearly as powerful and convincing as *showing* them.

Another expectation for you, and one that's also within your control, is for you to continue to hone your craft throughout your career. By that, we mean you should constantly look for ways to improve your lessons. If you find yourself teaching the same lesson the exact same way for years on end, you might very well want to take a hard look at yourself. Are you using outdated examples or references your students can't relate to? Are you coming across as going through the motions since you're bored with the lesson? It never hurts to try something new if you think it'll improve your instruction. Once again, you're not looking for the "perfect" lesson, but it is ok to change your routine to stimulate your own enthusiasm a bit. Other teachers might tell you you're working too hard or trying to reinvent the wheel, but remember that although you can't do anything about other teachers you can look in the mirror and do something about yourself.

A final aspect of teaching, and one that's also within our individual control, is how we communicate with students. Fundamentally, remember that you are a public speaker. Pay close attention to your enunciation and pacing of speech. Record yourself and listen carefully. Do you rush through your sentences? Are you hard to understand? Do you have quirks of speech, such as saying "like," "um," or "ah" too often? Do you project your voice so the kids in the back of the classroom can hear you? We all have idiosyncrasies in our speech, so it's wise to determine if you have any that might detract from your effectiveness as a teacher. One common verbal tic, for example, is the high rising terminal, also known as "uptalk" or "upspeak." A high rising terminal is simply raising the inflection of your voice at the end of a sentence, such as people do when they ask a question. Besides asking questions, people may also use a high rising terminal to signal that they aren't finished speaking, so it certainly has appropriate uses. Teachers should be aware, though, that a high rising terminal can also make them sound unsure of themselves or that they're seeking approval. When making a declarative statement, then, it's better to end with a downward inflection. Another verbal tic that might make you sound like you're seeking approval is saying "right?" at the end of every other sentence. It certainly has its place if you're checking for understanding, but be careful about overusing it. Besides being potentially annoying, its overuse can also interfere with what you're trying to say. Students may focus more on whether or not you're going to say "right" again than with actually listening to your lesson. They may even make a game out of counting the number of times you say it, which is counterproductive to your lesson. Focusing on verbal tics may sound trivial, but believe us when we say they can have a huge impact on your effectiveness as a teacher.

What do administrators control?

Another key component of the "system," and one over which teachers have no control, is the administrators. You'll see administrators every day, they certainly have a role to play in the day-to-day experience of the students, and they clearly impact your short-term and long-term job satisfaction. Despite their prominence, one thing that could improve right away is communication about what their role is. Some of their duties are very clear cut, such as attending IEP meetings and dealing with disciplinary referrals, but by and large, it's somewhat of a mystery what their true function is within the school. What impact, precisely, does an administrator have on educational outcomes (and how do we *know* that)? We think part of changing education for the better would be to have clear communication between the administrators and teachers as to how they fit together to work for the same goals. Administrators and teachers seem to work at cross purposes at times, and we believe administrators need to do a better job of explaining both their function and how they're supposed to improve teaching.

One clear example of how administrators fail to communicate properly are professional development (or "in-service") days. Professional development is run by administrators and, in theory, is a time for administrators to both present and explain their initiatives to the faculty. We pointed out in a previous chapter how professional development meetings tend to be very haphazard affairs, typically of little to no use in the classroom. The first problem with such meetings, and one that should be avoided, is a lack of real focus on concrete issues affecting students or teachers. Other teachers

SHOULD YOU BE A TEACHER?

have pointed out that all the focus was on some proposed "solution" to a problem that hadn't been identified. New programs would be introduced without any explanation of what problems they were supposed to address. In effect, then, a solution was being advanced for a problem that had yet been defined, which is the opposite of how things should've worked. You may be wondering how on earth such a basic sequence could be ignored, and we wish we had an answer for you. Instead of putting their efforts into identifying and framing a manageable problem in education, some districts focused their efforts on creating just the right educational vocabulary, as if just the right words would magically solve something. Why that was the case, we don't know. It is easy to see how such an approach is perpetuated, though. Since problems are never clearly and specifically identified, it's impossible to evaluate whether a course of action was effective since no one would know what "effective" was. In such a case, even if a situation actually got better, you couldn't be sure whether the implemented program was what caused the improvement or if was something else. With no way of keeping track of success or failure, then, new programs simply kept being churned out on a yearly or nearly yearly basis.

Another problem with professional development administrators should address is the procedure by which they're conducted. We've heard from a number of other teachers that, after being lectured on new or old educational jargon, teachers would be broken into groups to brainstorm ideas related to the presentation. Typically, no one in the group knew what was going on, but that didn't stop the activity from moving forward. Each group was given a big, white sheet of paper and a set of markers to jot down ideas. One person, typically a high school teacher, would say, "My printing isn't very good" and so another teacher would volunteer to do the writing. The group quickly broke into the one doing the writing, one or two people volunteering ideas, and everyone else socializing. Every now and then, an administrator would stop by, ask, "How's everything going?" and then move on. After a suitable time, the sheet of paper was taped to the wall and the

CAN EDUCATION BE "FIXED?"

groups would present their ideas. If this sounds very much like a bunch of high school kids doing group work, you're correct. Having no real focus and using the same procedure over and over again didn't create the most motivated "students" and certainly didn't lead to anything worthwhile. We don't know if this is widespread practice, but until some districts change the way they approach professional development activities, there's nothing you as a teacher can do about it.

How, then, can professional development be improved? One way to improve these meetings is to allow teachers to suggest the topics to be covered. One of the things we always wanted to see, since administrators seemed to have some esoteric idea of how to teach the perfect lesson, was an actual demonstration or two of how to conduct those perfect lessons. Such a demonstration would address any ambiguity and give teachers a much clearer idea of the expectations for their performance. The issue with such an approach, though, is administrators aren't teachers. They can certainly find fault in what teachers do but are unwilling or unable to demonstrate a better way of doing things. Until teachers see professional development days as of real use in the classroom, that's an area which can certainly be improved. Once again, though, the reality is you have no control over such things and must work within the system given you.

A note on educational research

Related to professional development, but also unfortunately outside a teacher's control, is the educational research upon which professional development is based. This is another area where administrators fall short and need to change. Some administrators seem to have an also almost kind of blind faith in educational research, even though such research at times was proven invalid and unreliable. There are many examples of research that led to poor classroom practice, but an easy example of poor research was the concept of open classrooms. "Research" showed not having walls in classrooms somehow was better for students, and one of us actually worked in a school that was originally built on that model. As any classroom teacher could've told you ahead of time, this experiment was an utter failure. Not having walls, particularly in a middle school, caused utter chaos, with students wandering about from area to area and the noise level from one class disturbing all the others. Being the adaptive creatures they are, teachers quickly began using file cabinets and book cases to create separate spaces for their students. Eventually, walls were put up to separate the classrooms so that the students could actually learn something. Open classrooms were one of those ideas that sounded good on paper and had the backing of educational research, but it quickly went south.

Although it may not sound like the most interesting thing to do on a Saturday night, you may want to check out some of that educational research for yourself. Statistics may not be your thing and you may be intimidated by them, but it's important you go to the actual evidence and not simply take an administrator's word for what a study says. We recommend starting with the background and methodology of the study. Pay particular attention to the sample size of the study and to what extent the school cited in the study compares to yours. For example, if you work in an inner-city high school with 2000 students and an average class size of 36, a study about a class of 8 gifted children in an elementary school with an enrollment of 300 may not be applicable at all to your situation. You'd be surprised how many times in our careers we heard of studies that had student sample sizes in the single digits. A smaller sample size doesn't automatically invalidate a study, of course, but it should lead you to question both how representative that sample is and look for supporting evidence.

Another consideration when reviewing educational research is how many times a study has been cited by others. From our experience, much of educational research out there simply reconfirms what another study has concluded. Replication of results has value, no doubt, but if a study cites thirty other studies as sources, it seems reasonable to expect those sources would each add something unique to the research. If you look through a study and notice it's never cited by anybody else, it's fair to wonder if that study has much real value. It may, but it's foolish to simply accept a study's conclusion without examining its methodology, overall conclusions, and sources. Remember, there are a lot of people out there who want to get a doctorate in education, so there tends to be a lot of duplicate research out there.

Administrators and student misbehavior

Perhaps the most frustrating element of teaching outside a teacher's control is student misbehavior. Misbehavior can take a variety of forms, ranging from passive resistance of ignoring you when you're trying to teach to talking when you're trying to talk to actual physical assault. Although relatively rare, physical assault is a reality for teachers. One of us actually worked with a woman who had her nose broken twice by students even though she was the nicest woman in the world. There are certain classroom management strategies you can use, but some students simply have to be handled by someone with greater authority, and this is where the administrators come in.

We're going to warn you ahead of time that administrators handling student behavior will be incredibly frustrating for you. In our careers, it was extremely rare for an administrator to support us when it came to the students, regardless of the issue. For example, one of us had a student who continually put his head down and tried to sleep in class, and despite several phone calls home, his behavior didn't change. Eventually, he was referred to an administrator. The administrator scolded us for not letting the child sleep. The administrator's rationale was that teenagers are typically sleep deprived and need to get proper rest. Of course, we have no doubt if this same administrator was conducting a formal observation, we would be severely criticized if we let students keep their heads down.

We realize administrators are under tremendous pressure not to discipline students or suspend them, but if students believe there are no consequences for their actions, then the school will become unmanage-able. We've certainly seen that in our careers. It's also frustrating knowing administrators will permit one student to disrupt, and sometimes prevent, the education of thirty-five other students. We realize dealing with one child who's hell-bent on preventing an entire class from learning is a steep challenge, but we can't simply allow it to happen. Administrators expect teachers to handle such misbehavior in the classroom, but there are always those students who are simply beyond the teacher's control. Administrators expect teachers to teach every student but typically don't give you the sup-port necessary to do so.

Fraudulent grades

One real reason education is "broken," and one very few people want to talk about, is the issue of student grades. In theory, teachers have complete control over grading, but that's not entirely the case. In some districts, for example, students are automatically given 50 percent on any assignment they put "legitimate effort" into. "Legitimate effort" may be nothing more than the student putting a name on the assignment and answering one question, whether right or wrong. If you find yourself in such a situation, you have no choice but to give a student half credit even if that student did virtually nothing on the assignment. You may also find yourself in a situation where an administrator simply won't accept grades that are accurate and fair. For example, we know of one principal who walked into a teacher meeting and declared, "Everybody passes." In that particular year, one student did fail, but that was only because she had attended a total of four days of school during the entire year. You can be the one pure-hearted teacher tilting against windmills, but you're not going to win that game if both the parent and the administrator are against you.

A teacher's grading system is also affected by the concept of social pro-motion. Both of us have seen students passed along simply because of their age. You may find yourself, for example, with a number of sixteen-year-old eighth graders. You may also have the experience of teaching repeat ninth grade students who failed ninth grade two or three times. The students were simply passed along, so it might be the case that you find yourself teaching an eleventh grade English class that has five or six ninth graders in it. As frustrating as the situation may be, the teacher has no control over such promotions, and it's fair to ask if such a practice benefits anybody involved.

A final issue with grading, and one also out of the teachers' control, is standardized testing. Looking at any data on standardized testing should raise a red flag with any thinking person. It's not our intention to single out any one district, but it's fair to question why some districts score so low on standardized tests. For example, if there's a school where the percentage of seniors demonstrating proficiency in reading or in math is in the single digits, how is it possible the graduation rates are, say, 80 percent or higher? This phenomenon should be investigated on a school-by-school basis to see what's going on, but it seems like there's no interest in doing so. For years, we were told the reason for low test scores on standardized test was "test anxiety," but no one ever gave us any evidence to support that claim or any argument as to why test anxiety would apply on a standardized test but not on a classroom test. We're not suggesting standardized tests be the sole measurement of achievement or whether or not a student graduates, but such a huge disparity between those test scores, classroom grades, and graduation rates should be examined.

What about the parents?

The most important people you'll deal with in terms of their influence on education, and the ones over which you'll have the least influence, are the parents. You may see them at Open House or communicate with them briefly by email, but chances are you'll never meet the majority of your students' parents. Don't underestimate their importance and impact, though. There are those who will support what you do whole-heartedly, those who support you in a lukewarm manner, those who are indifferent, those who see no real value in education for whatever reason, and those who're simply absent. As much as you can, communicate with parents, let them know what you're up to in class, and keep them abreast of any new developments in their child's life. Online resources make it easier than ever to keep parents informed, but don't be shy about picking up the telephone and contacting moms or dads. Parents, in the ideal world, should be your number one ally in educating their child.

How, specifically, can parents help their child's education and make your job more manageable? One thing is to stop treating them like greenhouse orchids that must be insulated against any discomfort or challenge. There are some parents who believe that any sort of anxiety or difficulty must be avoided at all costs and that their children must never know an unpleasant moment. That sort of attitude doesn't serve the child well in life, of course, because the world is filled with challenges and the parents won't, and shouldn't, be there at all times to shield their children. How that translates into the classroom is that some students are far too sensitive to some of the comments their teachers make. As a teacher, if you're addressing an entire classroom full of children you probably aren't thinking about any one child, in particular. Some children do tend to take everything you say personally, and they're very happy to complain to their parents about any perceived injustice. Parents would do well to understand that children, at times, misinterpret what adults say, overdramatize the importance of trivial things, and sometimes even distort the truth to make themselves look better in the eyes of their parents. This shouldn't be a shocking revelation to anyone, but you'd be surprised at the number of parents out there who take everything their child says on face value. You have no control over how parents treat and respond to their children, though. We point this out not to discourage you but to make you aware of how some parents view their role.

Another thing parents can do to help their child, and yet another thing out of a teacher's control, is to make it clear that education is important and worth working for. Some parents are perfectly happy with their child devoting hours a day to sports or video games but don't feel the same way about school work. Throughout our careers, we've seen far too many students taking their studies casually with the full blessing of the parents. We've seen various reasons for parental apathy or absence throughout our careers. Some parents fear their child won't like them if they insist that child work harder in school. We've often heard parents say, "My child is my best friend" and believe parents with that viewpoint aren't very likely to demand harder work from their child. Other parents did quite well for themselves despite lacking much formal education and figured their children would do the same. Some parents were simply overwhelmed by the demands of life. There are no doubt other reasons why parents didn't or couldn't see much need for education, but the point is that without a clear message of support being sent consistently in the home, your job as a teacher is going to be extremely difficult. Supportive parents matter quite a bit, and you should be very thankful whenever you come across them.

What about the students?

One part of the system you'll actually be able to influence to a certain extent are the students. We don't want to get too confident here because, ultimately, kids are kids. By that, we mean children don't generally thirst for education. Very few students sit at home weeping on a snow day because school has been canceled. Such children do exist, but they are a rarity. Our point is that kids will normally show at least some sort of reluctance to working on their education, and at times will even show open resistance. Pointing these things out is in no way a criticism of younger people because they're going through a lot in their lives in terms of their changing social and physical development. The word "education" means to "lead forth," so in a sense, when you're "educating" someone, you're leading them from they are now to a (presumably) better place where general knowledge, reasoning, and communication skills are improved. Education, then, means you've been changed in some way or ways. If you haven't been changed by your school experience, then you simply haven't been educated. Part of that process is intellectual discomfort. Looking at new subjects you're unfamiliar with or looking at something you thought you knew from a different, more sophisticated perspective all involve challenging yourself, which isn't easy for adults, much less children who have a lot more things of immediate concern to them than education.

How then can we influence our students to at least see some benefit in their education? Quite frankly, as a teacher you're going to be responsible for "selling" your subject to your students. Kids don't mind working hard at sports, and practicing sports certainly isn't a comfortable experience. The kids are willing to put up with that experience, though, because of various reasons, one of which is they have a sense of social bonding with their teammates. It's also the case they feel they're accomplishing something, whether it's winning a game or match or seeing themselves run faster, jump higher, or have some sort of demonstrable change in how they perform. If nothing else, then, you should be able to justify to your students why they should put in the effort learning your subject. By way of illustration, it's important to study U.S. history because history is the evidence by which we judge what's going on today. If we know our history, we have some of the combined wisdom of our grandparents, great grandparents, and so on without having to take all the lumps they did in order to get that experience. Many of the so-called brilliant ideas that people want to try today have already been tried and failed multiple times in our nation's past. We would save ourselves time and tears if we realized that and we wouldn't get fooled so often by people who promise us heaven but deliver something else. No one wants to be a simpleton, so a proper explanation of how knowledge of history can prevent that very thing can be quite effective for your students. Regardless of the subject you teach, you should be able to provide a similar justification for the effort involved in knowing that subject.

Public misperceptions about education

Although we have no specific data to back up our claim, our impression is that the level of teacher contempt has gotten worse through our careers and the general public doesn't think teachers are as worthy of respect as they once were. In fact, many of the teachers we knew who left teaching cited both a lack of support and a lack of respect from students, parents, and administrators. Students and parents are far more likely to argue against a grade these days than they were before, and statements made by the students, administrators, or parents have become more direct and far more personal. Casual examination of the topic, even, seems to support our point. For example, how many times have we heard people "joke" about us having "three months off during the summer" or make cracks about the number of hours we work per week. Even on TV, there seems to be a casualness about being a teacher, with characters who have no background at all in education suddenly "going back into teaching" with no effort or trouble. People certainly make jokes about other professions, such as lawyers, but it seems to us there's always a hint of resentment in such jokes and they've gotten more frequent over the years.

There also seems to have been a shift in the attitude toward teacher compensation, particularly salary. For years, it was common for us to hear how we weren't being paid enough. Toward the end of our careers, though, it seemed a harder look was being taken at teacher salary. Specifically, people began comparing a teacher's salary to the median household income of a district, with the implication being there was an inherent unfairness in how much teachers made. Such comparisons, though seemingly growing in frequency, are wholly inappropriate. A huge issue with comparing median household income to a teacher's salary is that a "household" can be defined in a number of ways. An unemployed twenty-year-old with three kids and two forty-five-year-old lawyers with two students in high school are all households of four, but we'd expect their income and wealth to be very different. The same is true of a retired couple living on investments and Social

Security versus a couple of forty-five-year-old plumbers with no children. Both are two-person households, but we wouldn't expect their salaries, income, or wealth to be the same. Since households can be substantially different, it isn't helpful making generalized one-to-one comparisons unless you know more about them.

Even if it was possible to ascertain how a teacher's salary compares to the average salary in the district, what, then, should we do? Should teacher salaries be tied to the median household income in the district? What about income disparities among districts? Do you really want the lowest paid teachers working in lower-income districts, many of whom have children who need the very best teachers? Do you want teachers in higher-income districts making wildly higher salaries than their counterparts in other districts? Obviously, that kind of approach isn't workable, so we don't see the value in focusing on such lines of thinking in the first place.

Another public misperception about education that seems to be out there is that students today are taught exactly the same way their parents were. Doing our careers, we heard numerous times that, "schools are still using the same old teaching methods," which we assume means students are being asked to memorize random facts and simply regurgitate them on the test. If you've been through education program, you know nothing could be further from the truth. In fact, if all you did was have your students memorize random facts for a test or pass out worksheets all day, the administration would nail you to the wall. Today, teachers are expected to use a variety of different instructional methods to reach as many different learners as possible, so the idea of the one-size-fits-all teaching method simply isn't the reality in today's classroom.

A final misperception we wanted to highlight is the argument that "the old teaching methods won't work with today's students." We think that assertion is complete nonsense and some old teaching methods are as fresh now as they were centuries ago. We base that assertion on the assumption that being a good student today isn't a whole lot different than being a good student in the 16th century. Good students are willing to learn, disciplined enough to study, and relate what they're learning to what it is they already know. They also keep an open mind and are humble enough to acknowledge they don't know everything. Those sorts of qualities are timeless, and so any instructional strategy that capitalizes on them is effective, regardless of whether it was used with your grandparents or your children. We also base our faith in some of those old teaching methods on the fact that we were taught using those methods! Today, for example, lecture is considered an ineffective teaching strategy by a lot of educational theorists. If that were truly the case, then most of our high school classes and virtually all of our college and graduate classes were ineffective.

A great example of an old teaching method that's still relevant today is the Socratic Method. In this method, the teacher asks a series of probing questions that challenge students to think about what they and other students believe and why they believe it. It models how to think critically about the subject and gives the students practice in doing so. Thinking about what you believe and why, listening to others, understanding others, and evaluating what others say is how to have a civil conversation and find common ground, so we believe it's a critical skill for our students to develop and will never be outdated. The Socratic Method has fallen out of favor, though, because it requires teachers to be trained on how to ask quality questions and how to be flexible in posing those questions. It also is a style that can be quite foreign to students and may take them getting some used to. Further, administrators and parents tend to frown upon this method because it makes students uncomfortable since they're forced to talk in front of others. It's interesting to us that no parent would ever be happy with a coach allowing the players to sleepwalk through a practice, but they seem perfectly fine with letting a teacher do so during an academic class.

What's ironic about rejecting something like the Socratic Method is that the method is directly in line with modern educational theory. For example, educational theorists have identified that formative assessments are vital in the instruction process. A formative assessment is anything that lets you know your students understand the material before you actually test them on it. If you ask your students probing questions and ask them to elaborate on their answers, you're doing a formative assessment, and an extremely effective one. Trust us, if you use the Socratic Method in a classroom, you'll know within a couple of minutes whether or not your students are truly understanding the material at a proper depth. Yes, it is uncomfortable for students to be put on the spot in front of others and having to actually think and articulate their views, but nobody said school was supposed to be fun or easy!

Concluding thoughts

There's no dearth of theories on what we need to address to "fix" education, but we would caution you against accepting any generalized, simplistic explanation for any complex, multi-faceted issue. For example, poverty is often cited as an issue holding students back, but there's a lot more complexity to the issue than simply saying the word "poverty." It's silly to think that all poor people are the same, but some educational pundits act as if they were. A thirty-year-old single mother who dropped out of high school and is living below the poverty line, for example, isn't in the same situation as a forty-year-old married couple with a child living below the poverty line. In this particular case, poverty is standing in proxy for something else, namely, a single-parent family versus a two-parent family. That statement is a no way meant to disparage or criticize single parents, but it is the truth that children raised in single-parent households tend not to do as well academically as those raised in a two-parent home. There are a variety of reasons for that, and there are also certainly exceptions to that generalization, but the point is there are multiple factors that go into poor academic performance, not all of them necessarily tied to poverty.

If we can't start improving education by looking at global problems that are either ill-defined or hard to grasp, where should we start? As teachers, our focus should be on identifying and improving the things that we can and not getting lost looking for some perfect solution that will never be found. Specifically, our focus should be on our individual students, not society as a whole or groups within that society. Once again, we are treading on dangerous ground because of the political and cultural conflicts going on within our society. Eradicating inequality between groups is something people put a high priority on, but we must recognize our ability to affect it is extremely limited. It's silly to think everyone should be equally good at math or reading just as it's silly to think that everyone should be equal in athletic ability, mechanical skill, or artistic skill. A casual look at the world around us should tell us that. A student who scores in the 3rd percentile of reading comprehension will never have the ability to read and comprehend a complex text as a student in the 97th percentile of reading ability. It's not a criticism of individual students or a judgment about their worth as people, it's simply a factual statement about their abilities. We should certainly still be concerned about inequality, but our focus should be on how to help students maximize their own abilities and interests.

Finally, we should never forget to emphasize the benefits of being an educated person at every opportunity. Besides making students more marketable employees, education gives them knowledge of the world, helps them form opinions and develop a point of view instead of simply being told what to believe, allows them to judge incoming information so they are less susceptible to manipulation by a demagogue, and allows them to understand complex ideas and relationships. In addition to all those things, education adds to our enjoyment and appreciation of life, teaches us how to think, teaches us discipline and perseverance, piques our curiosity by exposing us to things we've never seen or heard before, and is essential to our system of government. If, in the end, you do decide to become a teacher, realize you're embarking on a journey that will change not only your students but you as well. And if you're very lucky, your influence can help shape a better future for everyone.